THE ECOLOGY OF TROUBLED CHILDREN

The Ecology of Troubled Children

Changing Children's Behavior by Changing the Places, Activities, and People in Their Lives

Richard L. Munger

Brookline Books

Copyright ©1998 by Richard L. Munger.

All rights reserved. No part of this work covered by the copyright hereon may be reproduced or used in any form or by any means—graphic, electronic, or mechanical, including photocopying, recording, taping, or information storage and retrieval systems—without the permission of the publisher.

ISBN 1-57129-050-8

Library of Congress Cataloging-In-Publication Data
Munger, Richard L., 1951-
    The ecology of troubled children : changing children's behavior by changing the places, activities, and people in their lives / Richard L. Munger.
        p.   cm.
    Includes bibliographical references and index.
    ISBN 1-57129-050-8 (pbk.)
    1. Problem children--Behavior modification. 2. Ecopsychiatry.
I. Title.
RJ506.P63M863   1998
618.92'89--dc21   98-10467
                                                                                                           CIP

Cover design, book design and typography by Erica L. Schultz.

Printed in USA by
10 9 8 7 6 5 4 3 2 1

Published by
BROOKLINE BOOKS
P.O. Box 1047
Cambridge, Massachusetts 02238
Order toll-free: 1-800-666-BOOK

*To Saul Cooper, Al Menlo,
Bill Morse, and Ruth Schelkun*

Special thanks to Tom Bensman and Amy Yeager for their splendid editorial assistance with this book.

Contents

	Preface xi	
1	**What is Environmental Intervention?** 1	
	Historical Basis of the Ecological-Environmental Model 4	
	The Many Forms of Environmental Intervention 5	
	Figure 1-1: Nested Components of an Ecosystem 6	
	Scientific Support for Environmental Influences on Behavior 7	
	How Environmental Intervention Fits into Other Therapies 9	
	Figure 1-2: Sample Continuum of Interventions and Their Emphasis on Environmental Components 10	
2	**Basic Concepts and Principles in Environmental Ecology** ... 19	
	Environmental Intervention as "Zookeeping" 20	
	Domains of the Environment 21	
	Natural Therapy System 23	
	Everything Is Connected to Everything Else 25	
	Environmental Trajectories 25	
	Figure 2-1: Environmental Trajectories of Anthony and Tony 27	
	Principles of Environmental Intervention 28	
	Figure 2-2: Anthony (Trajectory A) 29	
	Figure 2-2: Tony (Trajectory B) 30	
3	**Environmental Intervention and Contemporary Child Mental Health Care** 34	
	Children in Low-Income, Crisis-Prone, Multi-Problem Families 35	
	Children in Institutional Treatment 36	
	Individualized Care 39	
	Enabling and Empowerment 43	
	Managed Care 44	

4	**Developing Ecological Consciousness** 46
	Figure 4-1: Think of a Situation *51*
	Figure 4-2: The Eco-Map *54*
	Figure 4-3: The Personal Network *56*
	Conclusion 61
5	**The Environmental Status Exam for Intervention Planning** 63
	Figure 5-1: Benny—Age 11 .... *69*
	Case Analysis and Sample Environmental Support Plan 74
	Figure 5-2: Jason's Environmental Support Plan (ESP) *82*
	Conclusion 85
6	**Places As Resources** 86
	Home Environment 87
	Neighborhoods 93
	Workplace 95
	Churches and Other Religious Institutions 98
	Schools 100
	Figure 6-1: School Resources for Environmental Intervention *104*
	Conclusion 107
7	**Activities As Resources** 109
	Common Activities Among American Children 111
	Parents' Involvement in Arranging Activities 114
	Professionals' Involvement in Arranging Activities 118
	Community Involvement in Arranging Activities 121
	Youth Development Organizations 124
	Educational Benefits 132
	Conclusion 133
8	**People As Resources** 135
	Introduction to Social Support 136
	Influences on Social Support 140
	Consulting to Social Support Networks 145
	The Influence of Peers 157

9 Case Studies in Environmental Intervention 165

Henry: Male, Age 14 165

Figure 9-1: Henry *167*

Aaron: Male, Age 11 168

Figure 9-2: Aaron *169*

Tyronne: Male, Age 15 170

Figure 9-3: Tyronne *172*

Andrea: Female, Age 10 173

Figure 9-4: Andrea *175*

10 Future Directions 176

Glossary 179

References 188

Author Index 197

Subject Index 200

About the Author 205

Preface

Clinicians who are involved with the mental health of children and families would do well to arm themselves with the powerful tools of environmental approaches. Traditionally, mental health treatment approaches have been categorized into five broad areas: biological, psychodynamic, behavioral, cognitive, and family systems. Although theories of environmental intervention have been around for decades, only recently have workable applications of the theories emerged to make the viewpoint a viable force in therapeutic intervention.

Over the past two decades or so, numerous books and scores of professional articles have outlined new approaches to solving children's problems through environmental intervention. Although recommendations for environmental intervention have been available for 30 years, little has been done to routinely disseminate environmental methods to clinicians. My earlier volume, *Child Mental Health Practice From the Ecological Perspective,* attempted to synthesize what was known in the field and to stimulate further advances in intervention. However, the book did not prove useful to front-line clinicians.

The purpose of this book is to provide an overview of the principles used in environmental intervention, especially as they apply to children with serious emotional disturbance. The book is intended to help mental health practitioners to better understand a child's environments, the impact of these environments on the child, and the best ways to create more supportive environments.

In this book, the practitioner will learn:

- what environmental intervention is;
- how to think about problems ecologically;

- the basic components of the environment;
- key concepts in environmental ecology;
- the importance of the "Environmental Status Exam" for planning interventions;
- how environments can be engineered to change children's behavior; and
- specific environmental principles that clinicians can use to help children.

This book, intended for a general audience of human service clinicians, summarizes the environmental ecology viewpoint. I have taken relatively complex material regarding social ecological theory and reduced it to a set of basic principles; these principles can be used to address the needs of family members in a way that increases the likelihood that interventions will have positive effects on the child and the family as a whole. There is no promise of easy shortcuts in these pages, but there should be sufficient information to make the transition from theory to practice.

I have tried to present the results of research and theoretical writings in such a way that the front-line clinician or student of human services can apply the concepts to his or her practice—regardless of his or her specialized background of knowledge and discipline. The term "clinician," as used here, refers to any professional who interprets information obtained through research in his or her discipline for the purpose of diagnosis and treatment. The material, therefore, will be relevant to several groups of professionals: (1) those who work with youth with serious emotional disturbance; (2) those who work in child welfare and protective services; (3) outpatient mental health staff who work in managed-care settings; (4) those who work in the juvenile justice system with conduct-disordered youth; (5) school staff, such as guidance counselors; and (6) those who work in programs using environmental approaches, such as Re-ED, community home-based services, wraparound programs, multisystemic approaches, and other "continuum of care" projects.

In sum, *The Ecology of Troubled Child*ren presents explicit, practical principles for assessing and intervening with children's environmental resources. The book is a process blueprint, not a panacea for all mental health problems; an additional viewpoint, not a replacement for current methods; an organized set of principles, not a recipe book.

1
What is Environmental Intervention?

Chapter Preview
- Defines "clinical environmental intervention"
- Identifies the historical roots of the model
- Gives examples of environmental intervention
- Gives examples of ecological research studies
- Shows how other therapeutic models fit into an environmental view

Traditionally, practitioners in the mental health field have relied heavily on person-based theories in assessing a client's problems. Consequently, psychological concepts have outnumbered and overshadowed environmental theories—not only in assessment activities, but also in the designing of interventions. One of the primary reasons for this imbalance has been the inherent difficulty of developing a coherent program of environmental interventions. Although person-based theories can be complex, the associated practical techniques and strategies used by clinicians are derived from a self-contained set of theoretical principles. Implementing environmental interventions, on the other hand, requires the clinician to assimilate knowledge of diverse theories, many of which were not developed with clinical intervention in mind (Tracy & McDonell, 1991).

The 1990s have brought increasing recognition within the field of mental health treatment that a person's environment is a critical factor in his or her mental health. Children and their families are embedded in a complex web of relationships—a web that touches on far more than just the interpersonal relationships among members of the immediate family. When the "big picture" of a child's (or anyone's) mental health is brought into focus, physical surroundings, social structures, and relationships with others outside the immediate family all come into view.

From this perspective, it becomes quite clear that it is rarely adequate or meaningful to assess a child's mental health without considering the environmental realm. To draw an analogy, in understanding language, when something is taken out of context, misunderstandings and other problems often follow. When an assessment of a child includes all levels of his or her environment—all strands of the web—then more information is available and more options for meaningful, successful intervention become apparent.

Most people probably associate the terms "ecology" and "environment" with biology and nature. The term "ecology" is commonly understood to refer to all the reciprocal and interrelated forces linking organisms and their environment. Plants, animals, climate, habitat, food chains, and natural resources—and the ways these factors interact with, influence, and are influenced by the existence of man and technology—are all woven together into the concept of ecology. The idea for an ecological perspective in mental health assessment and intervention actually derives from field biology. A field biologist who is interested in a particular organism or specimen adopts the entire biological community surrounding the subject as the object of study and the unit of analysis. Thus, the ecological mindset is that of the naturalist, exploring both the overall nature of the environment and the ways its components affect the functioning of the individual (Trickett & Schmid, 1993).

The use of the terms "ecological," "environmental," and "environmental ecology" has resulted in confusion about their differences. To think ecologically is to concentrate on the *interrelationships* between *all* levels that comprise an organism and its environment. In the case of a child, this means the child-as-individual (biological, intrapsychic, cognitive, and other factors), as well as intra- and extra-familial influences (including peer, school, neighborhood, community, and overarching institutional and cultural factors). "Environment," on the other hand, typically has come to mean only the extrafamilial factors and beyond, including the physical environment. "Environmental ecology," then, means understanding the interrelationships between environmental factors as they influence the child and his or her family.

Fine (1992) has noted that there is great linguistic diversity and conceptual complexity surrounding the attempts by theoreticians and practitioners to understand and intervene from an ecological-environmental perspective. Therefore, a definition of terms is a good place to begin:

> *Clinical environmental intervention* seeks to modify the ecology of relevant contexts and settings that shape the developmental pathways of children. The goals of environmental intervention are: 1) to modify aspects of the environment that may be developmentally hazardous and predispose children to acquire vulnerabilities and/or that precipitate the onset of adaptive difficulties; and 2) to enhance conditions in contexts and settings that increase the probability that children will "naturally" acquire the competencies and strengths that will make them more resilient in the face of life's challenges (adapted from Trickett & Schmid, 1993).

Defining a mental health problem in terms of both the person and pertinent environmental factors helps establish an expanded arena for intervention. That is, intervention can be directed toward the person, the environment (both social and nonsocial), or both the person and the environment at the same time. Regardless of the target, the crucial aspect of environmental intervention is the emphasis on promoting behavior change in the child's natural environment.

There are no widely applicable rules about the ideal social and physical environments for families; consequently, there is no one catch-all formula for facilitating environmental change. Rather, appropriate intervention strategies are tailored to the individual family's situation, the goals of intervention, and the form of psychotherapeutic services being delivered.

The effects of proper environmental intervention can be far-reaching. Quite apart from any direct effects that are planned for, implementing the right changes in the environment can also help a client achieve or maintain benefits from other psychotherapeutic interventions. The potential power of environmental strategies demands a broader view in planning mental health interventions. The focus must be not only on helping clients acquire new competencies in dealing with their environments, but also on shaping healthier, more supportive environments for clients and their families (Tracy & McDonell, 1991). In general, environmental interventions can be classified under four broad activities:

- Realigning existing environmental resources to make them more effective.
- Strengthening existing environmental resources to make them more supportive.
- Making environmental resources more accessible.
- Infusing the environment with new resources.

Historical Basis of the Ecological-Environmental Model

Bronfenbrenner (1979) was one of the first persons to elucidate an ecological model focused on mental health. He viewed a child's development as a function of complex interactions among systems and settings in which behaviors take place. He wrote:

> The ecology of human development involves the scientific study of the progressive, mutual accommodation between an active, growing human being and the changing properties of the immediate settings in which the developing person lives, as this process is affected by relations between these settings, and by the larger contexts in which these settings are embedded (Bronfenbrenner, 1979, p. 6).

Bronfenbrenner conceptualized four levels, or spheres, of social context as a means of organizing all the behavior-influencing factors in an individual's environment. This convenient model is still popular today.

The first sphere is the *microsystem*, which represents the predominant social structure for every child—the immediate family.

An individual's behavior is a reflection not only of the interrelationships between the individual and the various settings encountered, but also of the interrelationships among the settings themselves. Hence, the focus at the second level, the *mesosystem*, is on the combined impact of multiple systems (best friends, teachers, extended families) or the influences among microsystems. For example, parent-child interactions can influence the child's adaptation in the peer group or in the classroom.

The third sphere of Bronfenbrenner's model, the *exosystem*, involves any settings that influence a child's development but in which the child plays no direct role. Prime examples of settings at this level are parents' workplaces, which can have a profound impact on a child. Other entities often found in the exosystem are the local school board, the zoning commission, and a school class attended by an older sibling.

The all-encompassing outer sphere is called the *macrosystem*. The inclusion of this level reflects an acknowledgment that the microsystem, the mesosystem, and the exosystem are embedded within a set of ideological and institutional patterns of a particular culture or subculture. What's more, everything exists within a particular historical time period that contributes its own unique influences.

Bronfenbrenner's hierarchical model, illustrated in Figure 1-1 (p. 6), offers a way of understanding the processes by which environmental factors influence behavior, by tracing them through the ecological levels—from concrete and immediate settings to more abstract values and social contexts.

The Many Forms of Environmental Intervention

Often, there are fairly simple, straightforward ways to create responsive, supportive environments that meet children's behavioral needs. It is being done every day, everywhere, in thousands of ways. Examples of common interventions in several domains of a child's life include:

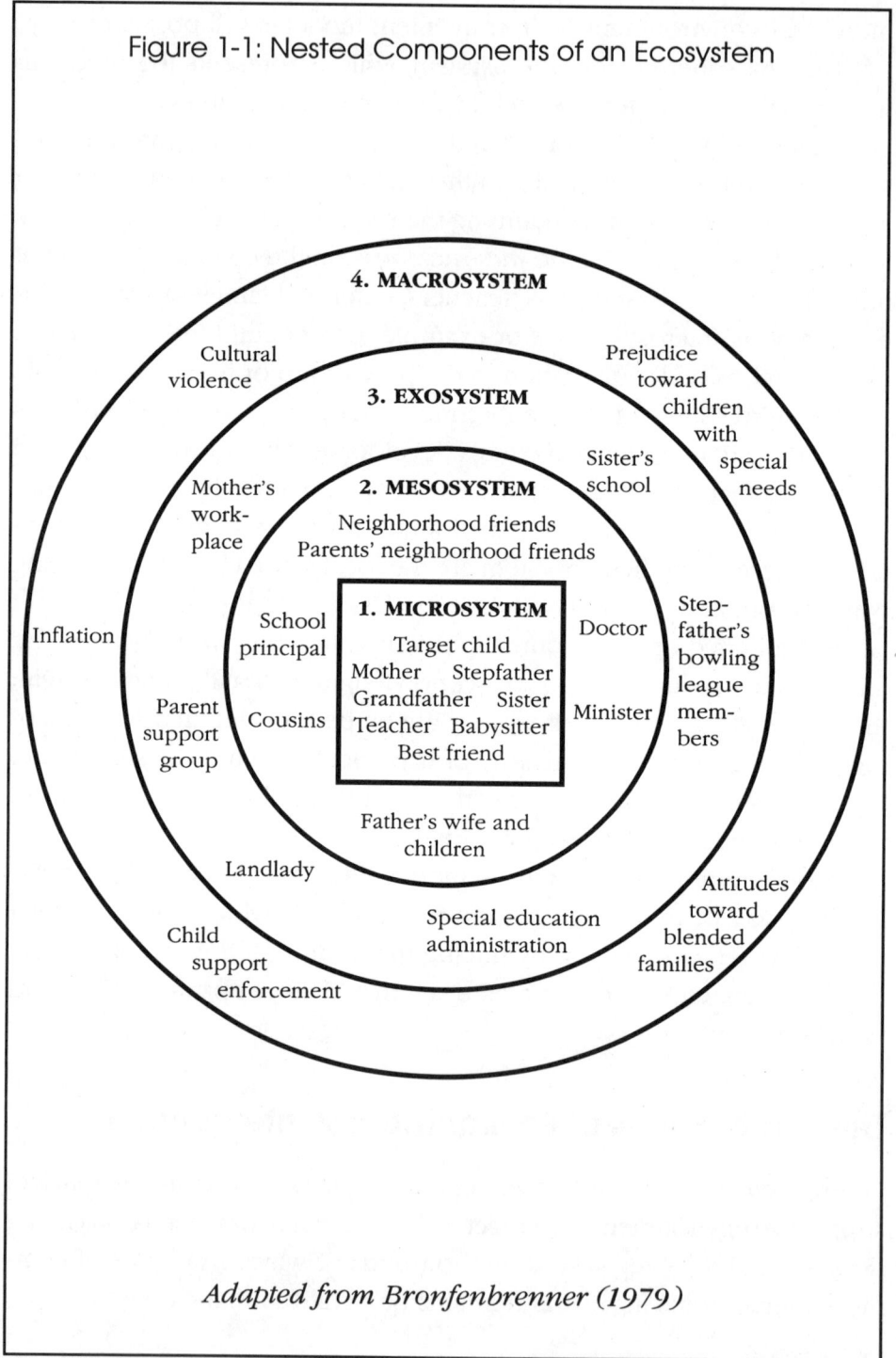

Figure 1-1: Nested Components of an Ecosystem

Adapted from Bronfenbrenner (1979)

Schools:
- Alternative learning environments (e.g., open classrooms, team teaching, etc.)
- Peer tutoring
- Adult mentoring
- Extracurricular activities
- High expectations for students' use of discretionary time

Churches/Synagogues:
- Parsonage/rectory available for respite for a child in crisis
- Youth groups and summer camps
- On-call emotional support from rabbi, priest, or minister
- Help/advocacy for a family trying to access services
- Congregation as extended family

Neighborhoods:
- Opportunities for informal employment provided by merchants
- Recreational opportunities nearby
- Helpful neighbors
- Improved housing opportunities
- Police informally help watch children

Communities:
- Job apprenticeships
- Youth clubs (adult-supervised activities)
- Organized sports
- Self-help groups
- Financial help from service clubs during a family crisis

Scientific Support for Environmental Influences on Behavior

Research on the interactions between people and their physical and social environments is highly relevant to mental health clinicians who use environmental approaches. Each of the studies summarized below demonstrated that the behavior of individuals is markedly affected by the environments in which they or their families are placed:

- Browne and Francis (1993) investigated whether adolescent participants in school-sponsored, organized sports (baseball, for example) experience greater feelings of social competence than their peers who choose to participate in more independent, less traditional sports, such as skateboarding. They found that positive outcomes (e.g., higher self-esteem, popularity among peers) can accompany participation in both traditional *and* nontraditional sports—even those often devalued by adults, such as skateboarding.
- Inman (cited in Meer, 1986) reported that 50% of families living in houses with only one bathroom suffered significant family stress, with the lack of privacy being a contributing factor. Only 14% of families living in houses with two or more bathrooms reported significant family stress.
- In a study of at-risk youths, Pastore and Newman (1990) found that increases in a family's active-recreational orientation (i.e., participation in social/recreational activities) correlated with significant decreases in the at-risk youth's internalization problems (worry, anxiety, depression, and low self-esteem). Increases in family active-recreational orientation were also directly related to improvement in the at-risk youth's self-control.
- A study by Shinn and colleagues (1989) looked at the flexibility allowed by employers in scheduling job hours for full-time employees with children. Perceived flexibility of job schedule was found to correlate with the well-being of the working parents.
- Trulson (1986) studied the influence of extracurricular activities on teenage delinquents. One group received full training in Tae Kwon Do, a Korean martial art that blends philosophy and physical activity. Another group went through the physical part of the Tae Kwon Do system in a modernized, streamlined form, without the abstract philosophy and the practical psychology to which the Koreans attach so much importance. Members of the group that studied the full Korean martial arts tradition showed a distinct improvement in their social behavior, becoming less aggressive, less susceptible to stress, and more self-assured. Mem-

bers of the other group, who were deprived of the philosophical and psychological components of the system, showed a distinct regression, becoming more delinquent than they had been.
- Van Meter, Haynes, and Kropp (1987) studied parents who had a child removed from the home and placed into foster care. The study showed that mothers who failed to have their children returned from foster care were likely to have only one or two friends, but to see these friends very frequently. The researchers concluded that expectations of or encouragement from others to spend time with them provided those mothers with an alternative that was easier than working toward the goal of getting control of their own lives and family environment to facilitate the children's return from foster care.
- Adolescents who attended church frequently and whose religious beliefs helped provide meaning for their lives were found to have lower depression scores than their classmates without these characteristics (Wright, Frost, & Wisecarver, 1993).

How Environmental Intervention Fits into Other Therapies

Although environmental intervention has long been downplayed as a treatment strategy, mental health intervention is never implemented to the *total* exclusion of the client's environment. Figure 1-2 (p. 10) provides a general overview of just how much the concepts of environmental ecology factor into various therapeutic approaches. The figure is followed by a discussion of the environmental aspects of each approach, along with examples. Keep in mind that the various therapeutic approaches are not discrete models; they often overlap. And furthermore, the designated percentages of focus on the environment are rough approximations and useful only for general comparisons.

Figure 1-2: Sample Continuum of Interventions and Their Emphasis on Environmental Components

Percent of Focus on Environment	Type of Intervention	Examples
10%	Traditional therapeutic approaches	Psychotherapy (Reisman & Ribordy, 1993)
20%	Reintegration into the community during residential placement	Re-ED (Hobbs, 1982)
30%	Interventions that extend into the environment	Case management (Behar, Zipper, & Weil, 1994); Family systems therapy (Schwartzman, 1985)
50%	Integration of environmental changes into a therapeutic approach	Multisystemic therapy (Henggeler & Borduin, 1990); Homebuilders (Kinney, Haapala, & Booth, 1991); Family preservation (Wells & Biegel, 1991); Wraparound, individualized services (Burchard & Clarke, 1990)
70%	Interventions that emphasize the environment	Therapeutic case advocacy (Young, 1990); Home-based therapy (Tracy & McDonell, 1991); School-based collaboration (O'Callaghan, 1993); Family network therapy (Reuveni, 1979)
90%	Principally environmental intervention	Environmental ecology therapy (Munger, 1991)

Traditional Therapeutic Approaches (Psychotherapy)

In the field of child mental health, standard treatment methods are aimed at modifying the psychological factors that influence a child's behavior. These "inner" factors include the feelings, moods, thoughts, motives, self-concepts, and attitudes of the child, along with many other traits and dispositions (Reisman & Ribordy, 1993).

When practitioners of the more traditional psychotherapy approaches do consider "outer" factors (e.g., parents, family life, race relations, neighborhood conditions), it is mainly for the sake of interpretation and diagnosis. Treatment remains highly individualistic, consisting primarily of one-on-one sessions between the clinician and the child. As stated earlier, clinicians who use this traditional approach believe that when the inner factors are taken care of, desired changes in the outer factors will necessarily follow.

Reintegration into the Community During Residential Placement: Project Re-ED

Project Re-ED (for "re-education") is an approach developed by Nicholas Hobbs, whose book *The Troubled and Troubling Child* (1982) details this residential program and its ecological underpinnings.

When a child is referred to Re-ED, the clinician must first identify the child's entire social network. This is often accomplished through discussions with the child, the parent(s), and any public agencies involved with the family. Then the clinician needs to seek out and talk to all the people of importance in the child's network. The goal is to find the answers to two simple questions: (1) what are the difficulties in the relationships between the child and other members of the network, and (2) what can be done to eradicate, or at least minimize, those difficulties? With the information gathered from the key individuals in the network, the clinician can identify appropriate environmental supports to bring into the intervention.

Since the purpose of Re-ED is to modify the child's network to achieve a better fit with the child's needs, the emphasis is on the future. Rather than focusing on what might have happened in the past to cause a particular dysfunction (the strategy employed in most traditional psychotherapies), the clinician outlines what has to be done to bring the child's environment into congruence with the child and give stability to the entire system (Hobbs, 1982).

Interventions That Extend into the Environment

Case Management. A paradigm for a case manager might look something like this:

(1) Examine the child and construct a plan for intervention.
(2) Bring the child to the attention of the proper community agencies.
(3) Coordinate the intervention, keeping track of the child's progress (or regress).
(4) Maintain communication with the child, parent(s), and agencies, and promote communication among them.
(5) Note and act when additional services are needed.
(6) Provide necessary counsel to the child as the agencies perform their functions.
(7) After the intervention has ended, maintain contact with the child and the child's family, and be ready to move back in should a relapse occur (Behar et al., 1994).

Because case managers are not the primary hands-on people in the intervention, they are often viewed as being little more than onlookers and consultants. Successful environmental intervention, however, requires a more active role of case managers. Some experts believe that all mental health therapists would benefit from developing an overview of the community elements relevant to the treatment of a particular individual or family—that every therapist would do well to cultivate a "case management attitude" (Mannino & Shore, 1984).

Family Systems Therapy. The unifying belief among family systems therapists is that children are best understood and treated within the context of the environment in which they live (Schwartzman, 1985). This means analyzing and using the family, the school, and the community in the intervention. Although intervention with children was meant to involve all these elements, in practice most family systems therapy has focused almost exclusively on the family, without much consideration given to the broader environmental influences.

Integration of Environmental Changes into a Therapeutic Approach

Multisystemic Therapy. Henggeler and Borduin (1990) have described a new approach to traditional outpatient psychotherapy. Their "multisystemic therapy," a set of empirically derived intervention strategies, involves the community and acts to modify environmental conditions that are detrimental to a child's mental health. Assessment focuses on identifying critical elements of the child's and family's interactions with extrafamilial systems. The approach is truly multisystemic, drawing from such problem-focused treatment models as strategic family therapy, structural family therapy, behavioral parent training, and cognitive behavior therapy. This intervention is specifically designed to promote change within the child's natural environment.

Homebuilders. In the 1970s, a group of therapists in Tacoma, Washington, conceived a unique mental health service delivery strategy aimed at preventing family dissolution (Kinney et al., 1991). The program, called Homebuilders, staffs therapists on 24-hour standby, ready to be called to the homes of families in crisis to help prevent family breakups. In addition to helping resolve immediate crises, therapists may remain in the family's home for up to six weeks to help family members acquire skills in coping and crisis avoidance. Staff members work with around 20 families a year, or an average of about two per month.

Therapists who use the Homebuilders approach perform three essential functions. First, by modeling effective communication skills, the therapist helps the family members improve their own communication skills and reinforces the clients' newly acquired competencies. Until the family is confident in its ability to communicate, the therapist can advocate for family members needing support in communicating with children, siblings, or parents. Another primary task of the therapist is to instruct family members in ways to anticipate and prevent crisis recurrence. This effort is supported by improved communication. Replacing aggressiveness or hostility with assertiveness enables family members to get along while acknowledging individual territorial boundaries. One strategy that can be effective is to encourage family members to negotiate behavioral agreements or "contracts." The therapist's last essential function is to set up treatment mechanisms that will continue after the intervention ends. It is often appropriate to structure a network of community resources that family members can access to help them reach future goals.

Family Preservation. The family preservation approach is built around three primary goals: (1) to preserve the integrity of the family unit (this involves preventing the unnecessary placement of children in substitute care while simultaneously ensuring the safety of each child); (2) to develop a strong, ongoing community support system that links the family with appropriate community agencies and individuals; and (3) to increase the coping skills of the family and to enhance its capacity to function effectively in the community. Family preservation interventions generally conform to the following guidelines (Wells & Biegel, 1991):

- The intervention is delivered primarily in the family's home.
- Service delivery hours are flexible in order to meet the needs of families; 24-hour crisis intervention is available.
- Services are intensive, with therapists carrying client caseloads of only 2 to 3 families.
- The intervention usually is time-limited, typically ending after 2 to 4 months.
- Home-based services are multifaceted and include counseling, skill training, and assistance in obtaining and coordinating needed services, resources, and supports.

Wraparound, Individualized Services. Typically, mental health intervention involves placing children into pre-existing programs that offer the categorical services best suited to meeting their needs. Individualized services, on the other hand, involve customizing programs to fit and serve each child. An interdisciplinary team comes together to answer the question, "What does this child need so that he or she can get better?" The answer often leads to a creative combination of services and supports of all types for the child and the child's family. This, then, is the defining characteristic of wraparound, individualized interventions.

The assessment and planning process for individualized care involves examining needs across all life domains. These include: residential (the need for shelter); familial (may be a surrogate family); social (the need for friends and contact with other people); educational and/or vocational; medical; psychological/emotional; legal (especially for children with juvenile justice needs); safety-oriented (the need to be safe); and other life domain areas such as cultural/ethnic needs and community needs.

One of the first wraparound programs in the country was implemented in Alaska. For the Alaska Youth Initiative (AYI), meeting the individual needs of clients sometimes meant providing supported living (24-hour-a-day supports, in some cases). The group realized that traditional 50-minute outpatient sessions simply aren't adequate support for many troubled youths. AYI focused on "wrapping" residential and daily structure supports around youths to help them develop sustaining relationships and build sustainable lifestyles. The program also focused on minimizing the number of placement changes as a means of keeping the youths connected with their communities and preserving continuities in the youths' lives (Burchard & Clarke, 1990).

Interventions That Emphasize the Environment

Therapeutic Case Advocacy. The term "therapeutic case advocacy" was coined to represent the concept of a case management strategy more encompassing than traditional case coordination (Young, 1990). The implication of Young's approach is that to be successful, intervention must focus on the environment-as-solution rather than on the child-as-problem. This involves coordinating the efforts of formal organizations and natural supports to help bring about beneficial modifications in the child's dysfunctional behavior settings. The ultimate goal is to establish an individualized system of care that surrounds and supports both the child and the child's family. The case manager's efforts to individualize and restructure the child's environment are geared toward

> the recalibration of expectations, instruction, support, and reward in each sector of the child's environment encompassed by the system of care. These changes make the child's interaction with it more manageable; and that is intrinsically therapeutic (Young, 1990, p. 122).

Home-Based Therapy. Increasingly sophisticated techniques are being developed for this approach, which zeros in on helping a child's immediate family to provide a more supportive environment centered around the home. This strategy of intervening directly on behalf of the family's environment has been developed primarily through the work of Tracy and McDonell (1991). They have outlined specific practice principles to guide therapeutic efforts in evaluating and modifying both the social and the physical environments of a child's home and neighborhood.

In the social realm, one of the core elements of home-based therapy consists of home visits by the therapist. This in-the-field contact provides better access to all family members, particularly those who may be reluctant to participate in the intervention. It also gives the environmental interventionist an opportunity to establish contact with other natural helping networks composed of relatives, friends, and neighbors. In terms of the child's physical environment, home visits yield first-hand knowledge of various factors that would not be evident in office-based work, including housing, individual space, privacy, safety, noise, etc. Changing elements in the home physical environment often supports and reinforces the achievement of other family intervention goals.

School-Based Collaboration. The idea in this approach is to identify the principal members of the child's ecosystem and to transfer the responsibility for change to these front-line players (O'Callaghan, 1993). The planning for this form of collaboration comes from the school, when a child's Individualized Education Plan (IEP) is completed. The goals and advantages of including individuals from outside the family as major players in an intervention include the following:

- *Facilitating the coordination of work.* It is often the case in mental health interventions with children that several agencies or people are working separately—or at cross-purposes.
- *Achieving increased leverage with a child or family.* Each person involved with a child has a different relationship and type of influence on that child. Assembling all the influential people in a child's life is a way of covering all the bases in preparation for dealing with any possible circumstance.
- *Providing an opportunity for everyone to learn from each other.* A worker who has been isolated in one organization may learn more about the workings of the larger system (O'Callaghan, 1993).

Family Network Therapy. A family's entire social network can be used in providing help for a troubled child. Speck and Attneave (1973) and Rueveni (1979) rank among the leaders of those investigating strategies organized along these lines. One of the standards of their method is to involve as many people from the client's network as possible. Garrison (1981) and others departed from this approach by working with a specific subsystem (termed the "action social network") of perhaps only 20 or so people in the client's network. A very specific network has been used in some other cases, such as in the family/friend consultation session described by Haber (1987), which limits the core group to a rather small part of the entire family-social network.

One of the key characteristics of family network intervention is the extended, collaborative network that forms around the core group. Those who are recruited for an intervention often form their own networks by approaching relatives, friends, and neighbors, and the members of this network will act together in searching for new, helpful intervention measures. In this fashion, the intervention spreads outward, involving more and more people. This widespread web of support provides the most efficient means of changing negative associations and extending quick, on-the-spot support to the members of a troubled family undergoing stress (Rueveni, 1979).

Principally Environmental Intervention

The goal of the clinician in an environmental intervention is to access and intervene on behalf of the family's environment. The intervention accomplishes these goals through modifying specific elements of a child's environmental context that are identified as particularly salient to mastering the personal competencies associated with the child's inappropriate behaviors (Munger, 1991).

This type of intervention is based on the theory that there are no high-risk children, only high-risk circumstances. It is reducing the exposure of children to these high-risk circumstances, and increasing their exposure to developmentally enhancing conditions, that concerns the environmentally-focused clinician. A unique feature of environmental intervention is the use of places, activities, and people in the environment as both targets and resources for change.

2 Basic Concepts and Principles in Environmental Ecology

Chapter Preview
Key concepts in environmental ecology:
- Like zookeepers, ecologists try to create optimal environments for their "creatures"
- Environment is comprised of physical, social, and institutional dimensions
- A "natural therapy system" surrounds all human beings
- Everything in the environment is connected to everything else
- Trajectories are environmental pathways that influence behavior

17 principles of environmental ecology

This chapter identifies the basic concepts and principles that form the basis of environmental intervention. Although they have been separated and categorized here for the sake of simplicity and ease of learning, these concepts are not discrete. Often overlapping and interrelating, they are not "cornerstones" so much as concrete blocks that interlock to construct an entire foundation. These principles will reappear throughout the text in the discussions of assessment and intervention.

Environmental Intervention as "Zookeeping"

Wild animals in captivity live and flourish best when their environments approximate the natural surroundings from which they come. For instance, animals that naturally live on the plains are more healthy and contented when they are not confined to cages, but are placed in open areas where they can roam at will. Animals that live in caves or dens need a place of solitude where they can feel protected. The most successful zookeepers build the optimal environments for meeting the innate needs of those in their care. In this respect, mental health environmental ecologists share similar goals and methods with zookeepers.

Ironically, while zookeepers always have the mind-set of making environments to fit the animals, many mental health professionals lapse into the habit of trying to make human beings fit their environments. This is a direct consequence of our having developed some capacity to analyze the human mind and alter thought patterns and behavior patterns. Interventionists may misdirect their efforts at simply doing what they can do one-on-one with an individual, rather than stepping back to get a whole-system perspective. Questions that too often go unasked are: Does this particular person need to be changed, or is the underlying problem basically environmental? Can the desired behavior modification for this person be achieved by altering the environment to create a better fit between the individual and the environment? These questions deserve careful consideration, because intervening in the wrong way can do more harm than good.

Recognizing the environment as a flexible medium that can be altered to modify behavior is quite different from knowing what to do and where and when. It is important to understand *what it is* about an environment that engenders health, happiness, and balance. Just what are the characteristics of an environment that is supportive for human beings? Lee (1985) found that most individuals consider their environment supportive if it enables them to (1) accomplish the most critical tasks in their lives, (2) achieve a satisfactory threshold of enjoyable, fulfilling experiences on a regular basis, and (3) avoid undue stress and strain. Intervention, then, becomes a quest to eliminate factors in the environment that do not support these characteristics, and to strengthen or introduce factors that do support them.

Domains of the Environment

A logical question at this point would be: What comprises one's environment? Although technically the proper answer is "all that is perceived or thought of outside the individual," some categorization is helpful. In discussing and performing mental health assessments and interventions, it is useful to view the environment as a composite of three interrelated domains: physical, social, and institutional (Conyne & Clark, 1981). Each of these aspects is briefly explored below.

Physical Environment

The physical environment is made up of both natural elements (geography, weather, plants, animals, etc.) and manufactured elements (buildings, streets, clothing, appliances, etc.) that people experience by way of the five senses (Wohlwill, 1981). The physical environment can have profound effects on human behavior. In fact, certain perceptions or "physical situations" have been found to elicit fairly standard responses in different individuals. For example, studies show that parents in crowded homes tend to punish their children for misbehavior more severely than parents in less-crowded environments. Also, there appears to be a correlation between home discipline and school conduct, specifically between crowded homes and increased aggression in class or on the playground (Martin, 1975).

Social Environment

This is the "people aspect" of the total environment, comprised of both individuals and groups. An individual's behavior is quite naturally affected by other people, and the nature of relationships between people varies tremendously—from the intimacy that can characterize husband/wife or parent/child relationships to the formality more appropriate between bankers and clients. Group dynamics play an important part in this domain, also. For instance, the size of a school's population has been shown to influence children's behavior (Barker & Gump, 1964). Good students do especially well in small schools, but even marginal students profit from such institutions, partly because small schools encourage participation in school life to a greater extent than large schools.

Institutional Environment

This last subcategory of environment includes such things as legal systems, cultural norms, and the rules and regulations of society. In a way, this aspect of the environment provides the glue and grease that help individuals get along and navigate in the physical and social environments. Abiding by traffic laws, maintaining silence in libraries, paying taxes, following building evacuation procedures in emergencies—all these, and many more, fall under the heading of institutional environment. The focus in this domain is on the relationship between individuals, or groups of individuals, and nonpersonal controls. The nonpersonal controls and guidelines that undergird a culture's value system are necessary for people to develop healthy personalities and to become socially well-adjusted. When individuals know what others expect of them and what to expect of others in return, a society can function smoothly (Glassner & Freedman, 1979).

Modiying Settings in a Domain

These three environmental domains are fair game as tools or targets for the mental health professional involved in clinical environmental intervention. Factors in all of them may have to be modified, directly or indirectly, before an intervention is successful. An interventionist has the option of selecting, changing, or creating different settings in any or all of these environmental domains (Price, 1979).

In *setting selection,* the clinician, the child, or both, look at the child's environment to identify already existing settings that the child should maintain because they promise to be helpful in the future. *Setting change* involves looking into existing settings to gauge the extent to which any should be modified to become more congruent with the child's needs. Any setting of significance in the child's environment—whether it be familial, educational, recreational, social, or some other—should be "on the table" and eligible for change.

Sometimes clinicians find that a particular client need cannot be met in any existing setting in the client's environment. At other times an existing setting might be found to be particularly damaging to a client's well-being. In these situations it is usually prudent to establish a new setting that will function as a positive influence. *Setting creation* can help provide children with resources either lacking or insufficient in their old environments.

To summarize, a clinician must identify which variables in a child's environment affect the child's behavior, both deviant and desired. The goal then is to decide what settings will spur the child toward the specific behavior changes desired. Finally, decisions must be made about selecting, changing, and creating settings to support the intervention and improve the child's behavior.

Natural Therapy System

Clinicians who work with children experiencing mental health difficulties can take some comfort from two basic facts of nature: (1) all human beings are surrounded by "natural therapy systems," and (2) natural ecosystems are generally self-restoring. Most of the time, children are in a state of dynamic equilibrium with their environments. With appropriate support from family, friends, teachers, neighbors, and others, they are usually able to deal with any environmental demands that crop up and get on with their lives. However, this natural therapy system can break down and develop an impasse, resulting in the need to seek professional help for a problem (Becvar, Becvar, & Bender, 1982).

When presented with a child client, mental health professionals in community caregiving agencies must keep an ecological perspective: they must remember that the child is only one part of a larger network. This larger network—the child's natural therapy system—needs to be assisted with the impasse it has developed. Interventionists must be careful to avoid doing anything that would disconnect the child from the ecosystem's naturally restorative power. Ideally, clinicians would not implement any "therapy" but would only serve as consultants to the broader natural systems in the child's life. Generally, if the impasse can be resolved, natural "therapy" elements will be restored to their full supportive capabilities for the child.

Of course, a mental health professional attempting to help a child must first build a trusting relationship with that child to have any chance at success. However, there are dangers involved if the bonds developed between the caregiver and the child become too strong. For example, Fitzgerald and Illback (1993) found that over time, as interventionists provided intensive in-home services for children, the support from informal helpers—such as friends, neighbors, and extended family—diminished. Too often, therapists either consciously or unconsciously substitute themselves for vital linkages in the child's daily world (Combrinck-Graham, 1990). This can leave individuals more vulnerable, with a weakened natural support system, as the intervention program is gradually withdrawn.

In many, if not most, cases, mental health professionals would do well to relinquish their roles as experts upon whom therapeutic success solely depends. Implementing a treatment strategy that acknowledges and involves the natural helping systems in a child's environment is the logical thing to do. Certainly, some child behavior problems require the expertise and experience that only a child therapist can provide. However, it is equally true that some people who are integral components of the child's everyday environment have unique knowledge of the child—knowledge that qualifies them to be useful participants in the child's therapy. An effective clinical ecologist serves less as a therapist than as a consultant who orchestrates the relationships among the many domains of a child's life, all of which contribute to solving the child's problems (Combrinck-Graham, 1990).

Everything Is Connected to Everything Else

Charles Darwin described complex interrelationships among organisms and habitats (environments) as the "web of life." This analogy was well chosen because with environments, just as with spiders' webs, touching one strand causes the whole structure to shake. All ecological investigations and interventions are based on this concept (Catalano, 1979).

Environmental intervention in mental health works because of this web. A child can be reached by, and can benefit from, proper modifications at appropriate points in the child's environment. When any component of the system is altered through some intervention, changes are likely to occur elsewhere in the system. On the positive side, this means that improvement in any part of the system can benefit the entire system. If it is dealt with carefully, this interconnectedness can provide a tremendous boost to mental health interventions. On the other hand, this interconnectedness can cause careless or poorly planned interventions to have far-reaching and unforeseen negative effects. Clinicians must be aware of this and must handle this powerful therapeutic axiom by approaching interventions with the thoughtful probing of a chess player, anticipating the consequences of each move.

Environmental Trajectories

In the early 1960s, Americans huddled around television sets to watch the first space flights return to earth. Reporter Walter Cronkite described the tense moments of re-entry, when the space capsule had to penetrate the earth's atmosphere at a precise trajectory or, if its path veered only slightly, face fiery destruction. The *critical path,* or *trajectory,* meant a course with the proper angle for the crucial dynamics of flight to unfold—a corridor of safety.

Just as a space capsule must maneuver through the invisible forces of space, children must navigate their own life-spaces, or ecosystems. They, too, create their own pathways—some that spin off into positive opportunities, and others that lead to failure and negative outcomes. Finding the proper trajectories for children to move through their life spaces might be just as important as with a space capsule—especially for youths with serious emotional disturbances.

A behavior setting—that is a place where activities occur—exerts an *environmental press,* which is the combined influence of various forces working in a particular setting to shape the behavior of individuals in that setting. Environmental press arises from circumstances confronting and surrounding an individual—circumstances that generate psychosocial momentum tending to guide the individual in a particular direction (Garbarino, 1982). Intervention, then, emphasizes linking a youth with an environmental network of behavior settings that facilitate specific, desired behavior changes. Figure 2-1 depicts how the elements of particular settings, as a result of their positions in the ecosystem, influence behavioral outcomes. The case study that is illustrated is outlined below:

> Anthony is 13 years old and lives with four brothers and his single mother in a two-bedroom apartment. His mother has physically abused him in the past, and Anthony was once placed in a foster home for nine months. His mother has only one friend, a neighbor to whom she is very close, but the relationship limits her involvement with others. Unsuccessful in sports in a large, competitive junior high school, Anthony befriended several neighborhood boys who spend their after-school hours skateboarding. As a result, Anthony has begun skipping school and experimenting with drugs. Excessive TV viewing causes Anthony not to extend his friendship network. His mother works the 4 p.m. to midnight shift at a local hospital, which means that Anthony is usually unsupervised and has little opportunity for activities outside his neighborhood. Anthony has recently been arrested for breaking into a neighbor's house.
>
> Tony, whose background is *the same as Anthony's,* has a pet to care for after school. A neighbor, who breeds dogs, acts as a mentor and friend to him. He attends a small school, which needs every student to participate in activities in order to have sufficient manpower, and therefore involves Tony in school

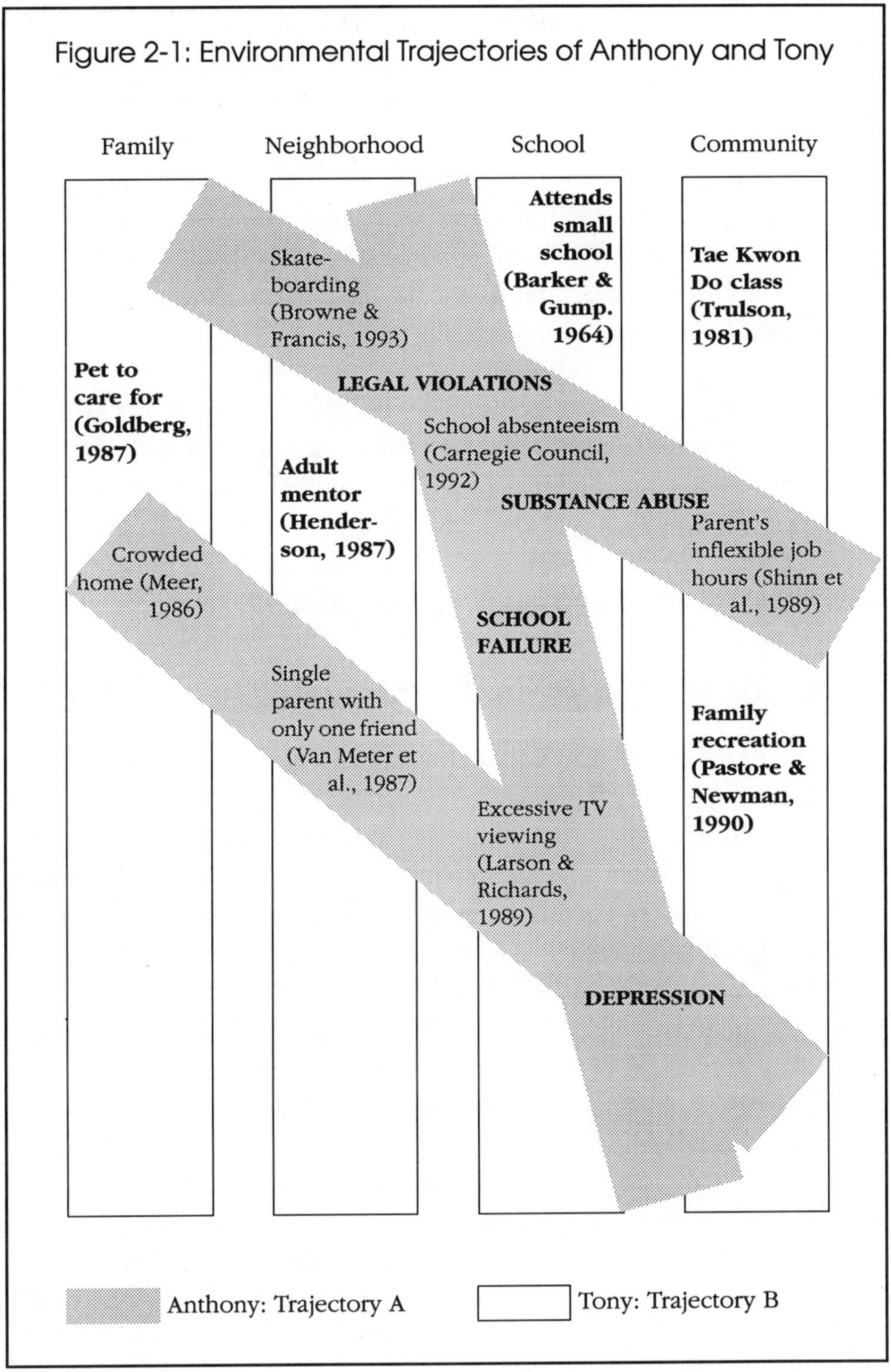

Basic Concepts and Principles in Environmental Ecology 27

Figure 2-1: Environmental Trajectories of Anthony and Tony

Columns: Family | Neighborhood | School | Community

Trajectory A (Anthony):
- Skateboarding (Browne & Francis, 1993) — Neighborhood
- Attends small school (Barker & Gump, 1964) — School
- Tae Kwon Do class (Trulson, 1981) — Community
- Adult mentor (Henderson, 1987) — Neighborhood
- Pet to care for (Goldberg, 1987) — Family
- Family recreation (Pastore & Newman, 1990) — Community

Trajectory B (Tony):
- Crowded home (Meer, 1986) — Family
- Single parent with only one friend (Van Meter et al., 1987) — Neighborhood
- School absenteeism (Carnegie Council, 1992) — School
- Parent's inflexible job hours (Shinn et al., 1989) — Community
- Excessive TV viewing (Larson & Richards, 1989) — School

Outcomes along Trajectory B: LEGAL VIOLATIONS, SUBSTANCE ABUSE, SCHOOL FAILURE, DEPRESSION

Legend: Anthony: Trajectory A | Tony: Trajectory B

plays, the band, and the soccer team. The school also encourages involvement in community activities and got Tony enrolled—with the help of funding from a local church—in a Tae Kwon Do class. The class has helped Tony with unresolved angry feelings he harbored because of his mother's physical abuse. His mother and two of Tony's brothers participate in a family softball club sponsored by the hospital—which offers flexible work hours for his mother, enabling her to broaden her friendship network.

Figure 2-1 summarizes the two very different outcomes for Anthony and Tony. While their backgrounds are identical, Anthony's environmental circumstances put him on negative pathways, while Tony's environments put him on a more positive trajectory. Figure 2-2 (p. 29) and Figure 2-3 (p. 30) illustrate the possible environmental, personal, and behavioral consequences of each environmental element.

Principles of Environmental Intervention

Henggeler (1991) has noted that some therapeutic techniques (for example, some behavioral and cognitive strategies) can be described and implemented in a fairly standardized fashion. But, he says, when dealing with complex social systems with many interacting factors contributing to behavior, protocol-based treatment is not realistic. In environmental intervention, it is necessary to describe intervention *principles*—as opposed to model techniques—which can be flexibly adapted according to the circumstances. This chapter concludes with a delineation of some of the key principles of clinical environmental intervention. The principles are discussed further in subsequent chapters, but this outline provides a synopsis.

- **Principle 1:** Understanding any individual's behavior requires first understanding the context within which the behavior occurs and the reciprocal influences among all of the contextual factors (Fine, 1992).

Basic Concepts and Principles in Environmental Ecology

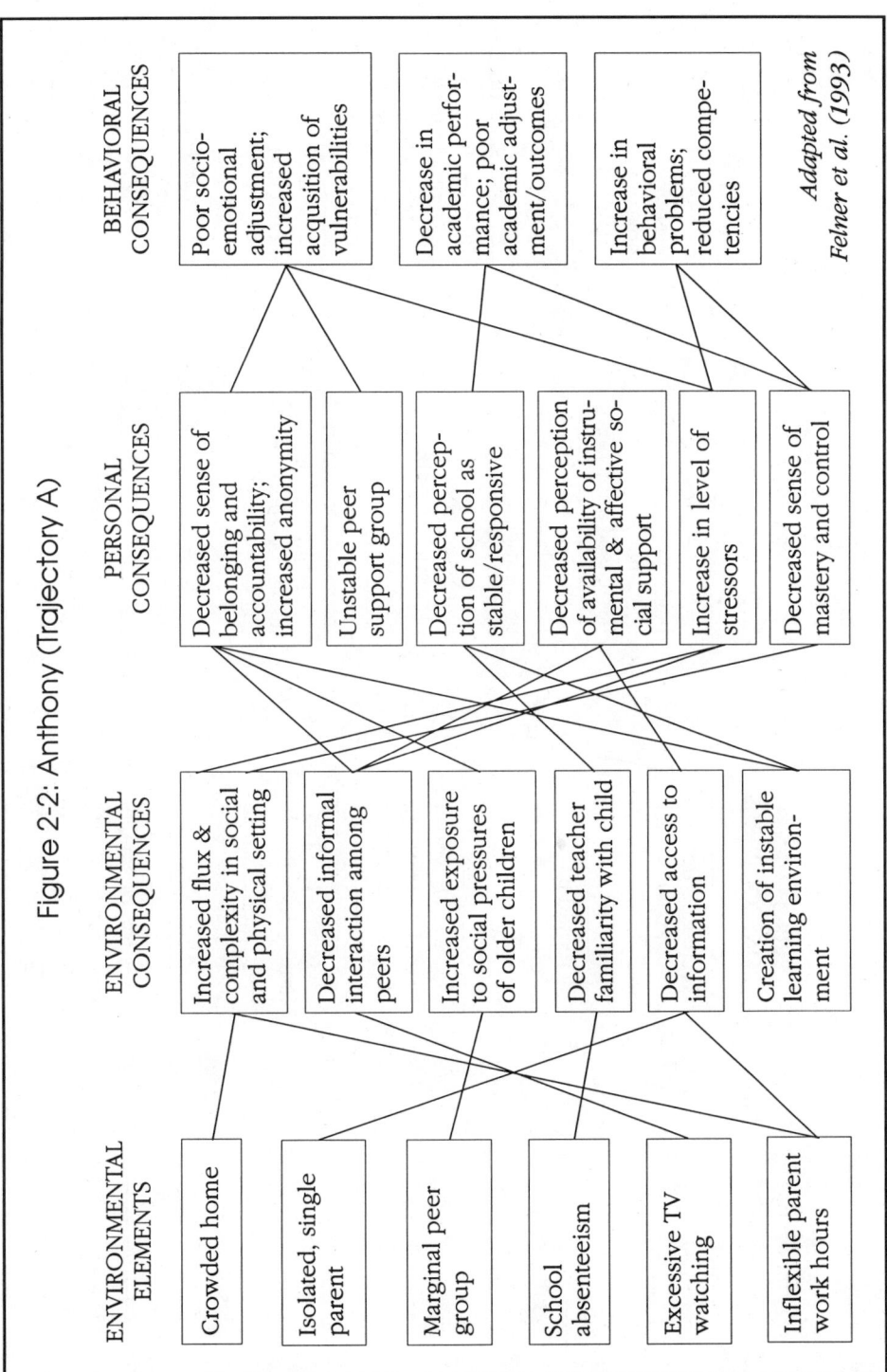

Figure 2-2: Anthony (Trajectory A)

Adapted from Felner et al. (1993)

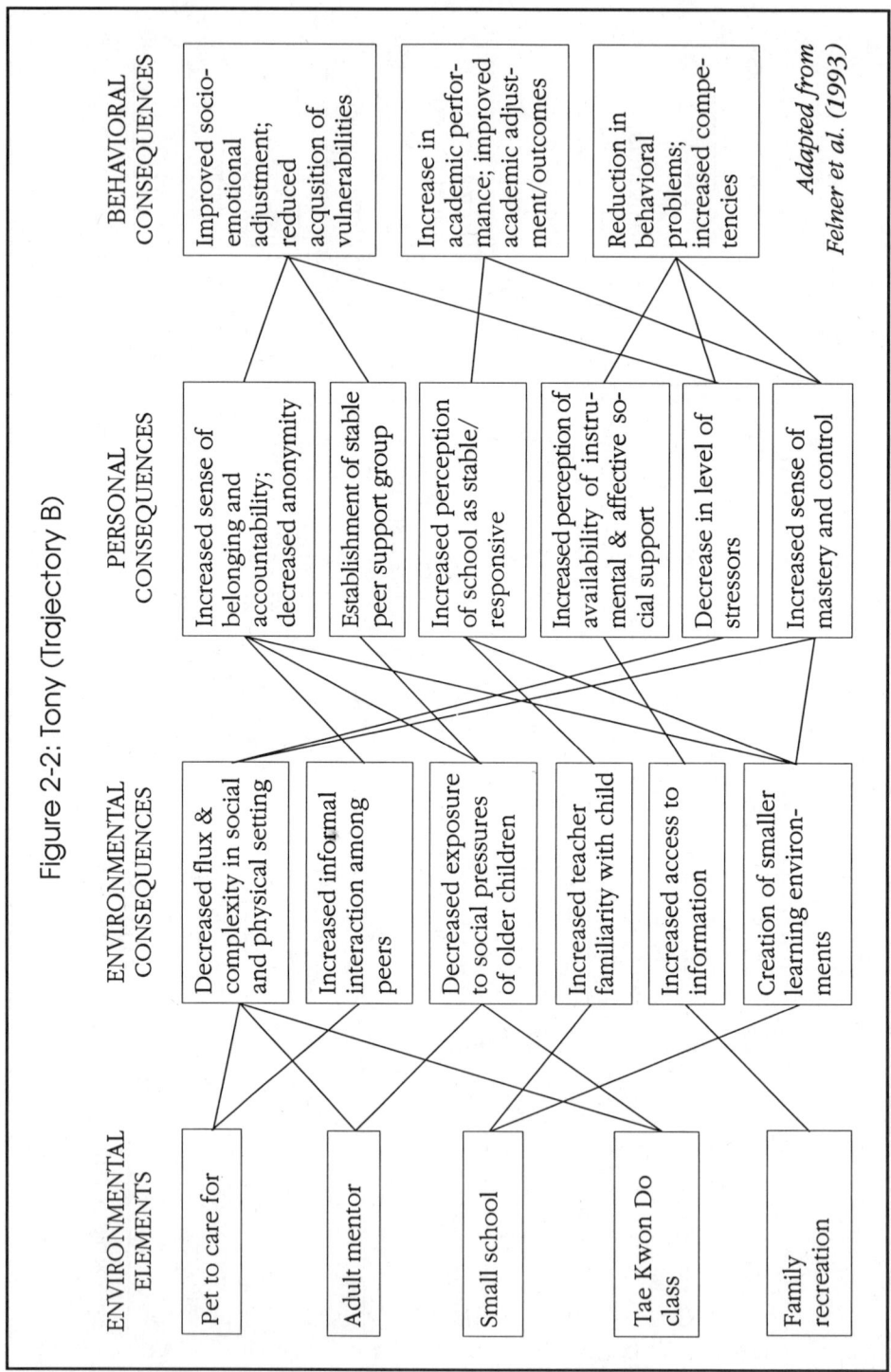

Figure 2-2: Tony (Trajectory B)

- **Principle 2:** Most child behavior problems do not stem from neurological, medical, or educational causes, but rather from inadequate environmental supports. In other words, the interface between the child and his or her environment is disturbed, not the child. Too often, interventions are focused on deficits in the child, when deficits in the environment may be the more serious problem (O'Callaghan, 1993).
- **Principle 3:** In the environmental view, disturbed or problem behavior is considered to be a symptom of a dysfunctional ecosystem, including the "fit" between the particular child and a particular setting. An ecological perspective fosters awareness of the match or mismatch between an individual and his or her environment (Fine, 1992).
- **Principle 4:** Many clinicians probably use an ecological orientation from time to time without calling it that. They attempt to view the total picture but often fail to consider the total breadth of environmental factors, thereby limiting the range of possible interventions. In contrast to a piecemeal approach, a comprehensive ecological approach opens the door for a variety of creative strategies to be used to effect change in the child's system and settings (Fine, 1992).
- **Principle 5:** It is much easier to help parents, teachers, and others in the child's life make changes in the child's environment than to bring about drastic change in the child's personality.
- **Principle 6:** A mental health professional of the ecological persuasion is not merely a family systems therapist, for he or she is limited neither to the family nor strictly to therapy (Combrinck-Graham, 1990).
- **Principle 7:** The mental health professional is not so much a therapist as a consultant to the many domains of a child's life, any or all of which can play a part in the solution of the child's problem (Combrinck-Graham, 1990). The consultative orientation is perhaps the single most important element of the ecological model. The perspective of a consultant allows the mental

health professional more flexibility and maneuverability in orchestrating interventions (Fine, 1992).

- **Principle 8:** A basic premise of the environmental viewpoint is that intervention produces broad-based social systems changes. The different settings in a child's environment are interdependent; events and changes in one area reverberate and produce changes in other areas. The interdependence principle states that because all aspects of the environment are interconnected, interventions that directly affect only certain aspects of the system ripple across other aspects, thereby bringing indirect consequences (Trickett & Schmid, 1993).
- **Principle 9:** The emphasis in interventions should be upon solutions rather than causes. Effective interventions that are both positive and proactive tend to focus on identifying choices and options for meeting needs rather than on placing blame or looking for reasons why things are not as they should be. Effective help-giving encourages and promotes moving from concerns to needs to actions as rapidly as possible (Dunst, Trivette, & Deal, 1988).
- **Principle 10:** The natural environmental resources in the child's life must be routinely brought into the intervention. The expertise of many people must be marshaled for the benefit of the child (Combrinck-Graham, 1990). A major goal of the environmental model is to increase the number of empowered caregivers and to create a collaborative spirit among them (O'Callaghan, 1993).
- **Principle 11:** An evaluation of the child and family should focus on strengths. With the parents, the aim is to find ways to recognize them as experts, based upon the assumption that all parents bring personal strengths and special expertise to childrearing.
- **Principle 12:** A major goal of environmental intervention is to put the child on a positive trajectory with regard to social relations and to give the family and other principal individuals in the child's life the motivation and ability to support that trajectory.

The key in the ecological viewpoint becomes identifying and enabling critical environmental trajectories in the child's life (Henggeler & Borduin, 1990).

- **Principle 13:** Compared to those who use more traditional mental health intervention strategies, the environmental interventionist adopts a more collaborative, non-hierarchical approach with clients and their families. The traditional boundary between professional provider and client is relaxed.
- **Principle 14:** Before parents are asked to carry out professionally prescribed, child-level interventions, efforts to meet other family-identified needs must be made in order to give parents the time and energy to be with their own children in an educational or therapeutic capacity (Dunst, Trivette, & Deal, 1988).
- **Principle 15:** Children do not belong in institutions such as psychiatric hospitals, large residential treatment centers, and training schools. These types of programs are unnecessary when families, including foster families, are given the support and resources they need to manage children (O'Callaghan, 1993).
- **Principle 16:** The clinician should always plan for the time that he or she will no longer be part of the system (Henggeler & Borduin, 1990).
- **Principle 17:** It is unlikely that one form of environmental intervention will be suitable for all clients (Tracy & McDonell, 1991).

3 Environmental Intervention and Contemporary Child Mental Health Care

Chapter Preview
Describes two difficult clinical populations where environmental methods may be especially useful:
- Low-income, multi-problem families
- Institutionalized children

Reviews several trends in the field:
- "CASSP"
- Individualized care
- Family empowerment
- Managed care

Any mental health intervention with children can differ substantially from the treatment of adults, because the environment is much more influential on children's behavior. Until their mid-teens (and often longer), people are, for the most part, confined within environments that dominate them and over which they have little control. Much of a child's behavior represents his or her attempts to gain some control over surroundings and situations. Certainly, the problems of children with serious emotional disturbances cannot be properly understood and effectively dealt with if the ecological elements are de-emphasized, or worse yet, ignored altogether. In fact, some would say that the more disturbed a child is, the greater the need for environmental changes (Schulman, 1979).

Two groups of children—those from low-income, crisis-prone, multi-problem families, and those with a history of removal from the home for institutional treatment—present particular challenges to standard mental health treatment methods. Intervention programs for these children often fail. Henggeler and Borduin (1990) contend that the primary reason for these poor results could be that traditional interventions tend to address only a few of the factors contributing to a youth's disturbed behavior. Environmental methods, with their wide net of involvement, offer hope for hitting on the right factors in any particular case and altering the trend of failure in child mental health interventions.

Children in Low-Income, Crisis-Prone, Multi-Problem Families

It is common knowledge that children in families with numerous crises and problems and a low income tend to exhibit behavioral problems at a higher-than-average rate. However, it is not so common to contend that the maladaptive behavior of youths in such situations is merely a symptom of a much broader-based disorder. Kraft and DeMaio (1982) were among the first to acknowledge that behavioral problems of youths in low-income families could be viewed as disruptions in the social system rather than as isolated personal or family problems. This perspective is classically ecological.

Kraft and DeMaio claim that the ultimate ecological problem is the family's poor connection with the network of resources provided by the community and society at large. They also warn,

> To focus on uncovering sensitive, anxiety-laden feelings without providing a payoff—increasing the availability of resources—could merely inflate expectations, remove a functioning defensive system, and result in even greater anxiety or more drastic coping mechanisms (1982, p. 133).

Treating only part of the problem can be worse than not intervening at all.

For the typical family described above, traditional interventions, such as weekly visits to a clinic or an agency, are inappropriate (and consequently ineffective). To begin with, such families often lack both a phone to make appointments and a means of transportation to get to the treatment facility. Those who manage to get past these obstacles and actually make it to a clinic may be uncomfortable with the clinical setting and treatment protocol. Some may even be frightened of being interviewed and advised on personal matters. What's more, people from these types of environments rarely seek help of their own free will. More often than not, they are pushed into treatment by somebody else—which can leave them feeling controlled from the outside, victimized by the process, and threatened by the authorities.

Unfortunately, the array of problems between these types of families and "the system" can result in the families' becoming virtually invisible to the agencies designed to help them. To be successful, intervention must improve family life by giving these families environmental supports, helping them see how these supports can diminish their periodic crises; and prompting them to take control of their lives. Outreach programs to families must stress that the solution for any family is to find its place (good fit) within the overall community environment (Clark, Zalis, & Sacco, 1982).

Children in Institutional Treatment

Institutionalization—removal from mainstream society and confinement in reform schools, psychiatric hospitals, and residential treatment centers—has been one of the most widely used forms of intervention for children with severe behavioral problems. Psychotherapeutic techniques, educational programs, and/or drugs are the agents of change most commonly employed in these institutions. The underlying philosophy for interventions of this nature is the individualistic theory that the children can be taught or coerced into modifying their behaviors, and that their personalities can be changed more or less permanently. The goal is for them to function adequately upon returning to their old environment or being placed in a new one.

The concept of extracting children from their natural settings and dropping them into unnatural, institutional environments in order to help them become better adjusted in the natural settings is grossly misguided. It is similar to a practice that was predominant a century ago, in which the mentally ill were sent to remote hospitals in the countryside as a refuge from the tribulations of daily life. Not surprisingly, institutionalization does not help individuals achieve a better fit with their natural environments. There is absolutely no empirical evidence that institutional treatment is effective (Saxe, Cross & Silverman, 1988). Its perpetuation appears more related to the convenience it provides professionals and the comfort it brings a public offended and frightened by aberrant behavior.

To realize the greatest benefits, children must be helped in the most normalized environment possible. Therapeutic supports must be put in place around children in their everyday environments so that they can learn to function where they need to function—in homes and classrooms and other settings in their worlds. It is only by establishing relationships and interacting in families, schools, neighborhoods, and the broader community that children grow and learn to be human beings. Consignment to an institution should be carefully examined with this in mind, for institutionalization, more than anything, removes the child from relationships and supports that are conducive to mental health (Swenson, 1979).

All human beings develop conditioned responses to environmental cues. To be fully successful, intervention must aim to alter the entire context of children's lives to get at the roots of behavioral problems and to change harmful or inappropriate conditioned responses. Community-based interventions provide the proper perspective for involving children's entire lives and for identifying and changing environmental conditions that adversely affect children's mental health. (Ironically, one such adverse condition could be institutionalization itself!) Lasting changes in children's behavior demand an understanding and manipulation of environmental factors; without ecological intervention, any changes are likely to be only temporary (Bechtel, 1984).

To summarize, the environmental dimension of many mental health problems renders them resistant to traditional psychotherapeutic techniques. The difficulties of children with serious emotional disturbances in institutions and in low-income, crisis-prone, multi-problem families reveal quite clearly the nature of the dilemma. The proper approach for the clinician is often to develop concrete, practical, environmental supports. Helping the families of these children improve their environments is essential for effective intervention on their behalf (Mannino & Shore, 1984).

Ecological theories certainly look promising in helping to serve historically "difficult" populations. Fortunately, ecological concepts are also being applied in other areas of mental health care. The following discussions focus on environmental aspects of the Child and Adolescent Service System Program, individualized care, enabling and empowerment, and managed care.

CASSP: Systems of Care

The Child and Adolescent Service System Program (CASSP), begun at the federal level in 1984, helped foster dramatic changes in our nation's child mental health system. Across the country, more and more programs have begun adopting the concept of community-based systems of care, on which CASSP is based.

Stroul and Friedman (1986) define a *system of care* as a comprehensive array of services that are organized into a coordinated network designed to meet the multiple and changing needs of children and adolescents with serious emotional disturbances. The concept encompasses traditional outpatient and inpatient services and much more, including case management, in-home and family preservation services, in-school support, day treatment, therapeutic foster care and group homes, crisis services, and respite care. One of the strengths of the system of care strategy is its diversity. Not all these services are provided by the mental health agency alone; instead, the system depends upon an integrated approach involving education, child welfare, juvenile justice, health, vocational and recreational agencies.

Developing community-based systems of mental health care is now seen as a national priority, and communities across the country are working toward establishing such systems. Unfortunately, there are some drawbacks to the implementation of systems of care. Katz-Leavy and her colleagues (1992) have noted two challenges in particular: (1) allocating available resources equitably and meaningfully among the various system-of-care components, and (2) developing resources sufficiently flexible for making individualized services possible. The first issue can be a logistical and political nightmare, and although the CASSP paradigm is technically sophisticated, it provides only a partial therapeutic design for dealing with complex ecosystems. The second issue hits at the core of such programs, for although the original "system of care" philosophy was built around the concept of *individualizing* services, this ideal often seems to be poorly implemented. There are exceptions, however, the most notable of which are the individualized systems of care developed in North Carolina's Willie M program, Chicago's Kaleidoscope program, the Alaska Youth Initiative, and Project Wraparound in Vermont.

Quite apart from its place in community-based systems of care, individualized care is becoming more and more popular in intervention strategies. An early, successful example is the Alaska Youth Initiative program. The following discussion takes a closer look at individualized care in general and the Alaska Youth Initiative in particular.

Individualized Care

Implementing a program of individualized care requires an ecological approach. An effective individualized approach must begin with a comprehensive, strengths-based assessment—one that examines all domains in the child's environment to discover the social ecology of behavior (Burchard & Clarke, 1990).

Like the assessment, the intervention itself must touch the child's whole world. A typical individualized program is a creative combination of all types of services, resources, and supports need by a child and the child's family. The comprehensive, strengths-based assessment becomes the key factor in the development of the individualized service plan for the child and family (Katz-Leavy, Lourie, Stroul, & Zeigler-Dendy, 1992).

To be truly individualized, a program must provide services that meet the specific needs of the child and family. This concept stands in direct opposition to the practice of merely plugging a client into a particular categorical label and intervention model. This is not to say that individualized interventions never involve traditional services such as psychotherapy, foster care, and medication. It does mean, however, that these services are brought into a program only when they can be tailored to help satisfy a specific need of the child or family (Burchard, Burchard, Sewell, & VanDenBurg, 1993). It also means that appropriate non-traditional strategies—such as hiring a special friend for the child, arranging for a staff member to live with a family, fixing the family's car or washing machine, or providing the family with a telephone—will be critical elements of the program.

One of the first individualized programs to achieve long-term success was the Alaska Youth Initiative, or AYI. A brief account of its history will help illustrate the goal of such programs: to design services that provide the client with a lifestyle that is both age- and culture-appropriate and that integrate the client (both physically and socially) into mainstream society as much as possible (Burchard et al., 1993).

Historically, Alaska sent most of its children with serious emotional disturbance to out-of-state residential programs. The common rationale provided by service vendors was that distant, highly restrictive placement was in the youth's best interest, meaning that if the youth remained in his or her community, then he or she would constitute a danger to self or others. However, careful examination of the evidence usually revealed that the issue boiled down to staffing, supervision, and staff skill problems (Burchard et al., 1993).

Over the last 40 years, evidence has accrued in the literature that aggregate and congregate living arrangements can do substantial harm to persons with disabilities and/or disturbances. It is now clearer than ever that placement of youth in aggregate care does not necessarily equal appropriate treatment. Problems with deviant modeling, lack of access to normative social networks, availability of contraband materials, victimization, undue stigma, and marked difficulty in program management—among several other problems—have all been amply documented. Nationally, the developmental disabilities service community has long articulated the value of mainstreaming persons with disabilities. For AYI, this came to mean that individualized care should employ practices that are not unduly invasive and that do not create lifestyles grossly different from those of the general culture. This feature meant that individualized care and resulting lifestyles should be as culturally, ethnically, and age-appropriate as could be arranged. AYI's own experience soon made clear that the odds of success were enhanced if youths were served away from other persons with marked disturbances or disabilities, and that each intervention should be considered as a "test" as much as possible:

> The test is not in the response to an individual service; rather, the test is in what the service system learns from the response. Our traditional approach is to bounce children around from one unsuccessful traditional program to another without learning much from the last experience that can be useful in planning the next. With the AYI approach, the child, along with a whole team, moves from one intervention to the next, each time learning more about what is likely to work. Often what works is very nontraditional, and, on occasion, maybe even bizarre (Burchard et al., 1993, p. vi).

Another strategy aimed at helping AYI youths build and maintain normative lifestyles was de-emphasizing the idea of services as a "cure" and, instead, emphasizing the development of service strategies that provide ongoing supports in the youths' natural environments. This alternative orientation grew out of an awareness that the literature offers few examples of severe emotional disturbance being "cured." Supported living, supported learning, and supported employment service strategies, on the other hand, all provide for ongoing maintenance of behavioral and quality-of-life gains in the least restrictive, most normative environments which can be arranged (Burchard et al., 1993).

The range of individualized services and supports in the AYI repertoire, many of which are primarily environmental in nature, has been outlined by Katz-Leavy et al. (1992):

- *Family Support and Sustenance.* Providing emergency assistance for the child, paying for utilities, paying to repair a car engine, paying for a telephone, paying for participation in Weight Watchers, etc.
- *Therapeutic Services.* Providing individual/family/group counseling, substance abuse services, a bilingual therapist or a therapist of color, respite care in or out of the home, etc.
- *School-Related Services.* Providing school consultation or an academic coach, utilizing behavioral aides or classroom companions at school, paying for school insurance for a classroom companion, buying a chemistry set for Christmas, etc.
- *Medical Services.* Providing needed medical evaluation, providing medical or dental care, paying for a tattoo removal, teaching sex education, teaching birth control, teaching medication management, etc.
- *Crisis Services.* Hiring a family member or a friend to provide crisis support, utilizing a behavioral aide in the child's home or in therapeutic foster care, teaching crisis management skills, etc.
- *Independent Living Services.* Helping to locate and rent an apartment, helping a youngster obtain Supplemental Security Income (SSI), hiring a professional roommate/mentor, providing a weekly allowance, teaching money management and budgeting, providing driving lessons, teaching meal preparation, teaching parenting skills, teaching housekeeping skills, purchasing a mobile home for a fire setter and providing 24-hour staff, etc.
- *Interpersonal and Recreational Skill Development.* Hiring a friend or finding a Big Brother, teaching social skills and problem-solving skills, or paying for a membership in an exercise gym, a YMCA membership, horseback riding lessons, art or music lessons, summer camp registration, a class trip, a fishing license, a bicycle, etc.
- *Vocational Services.* Providing job training, teaching good work

skills, providing a job coach, finding an apprenticeship, providing a mentor at the apprenticeship or other program, paying someone to hire the youth for a job, conducting a vocational skills assessment, etc.
- *Additional Reinforcers.* Purchasing reinforcers including items such as a radio, makeup, clothing, a punching bag, a skateboard, trips, dates or activities, photographs or teen magazines, etc. (Katz-Leavy et al., 1992, pp. 18-19).

Enabling and Empowerment

Mental health professionals are only too aware that intervention can have both positive and negative consequences. To increase the odds that a treatment program promotes healthy parent, family, and child functioning, caregivers must give as much attention to *how* support is provided as they do to *what* support is provided. It is not simply a matter of whether or not the family's or child's needs are met; the *manner* in which their needs are met can be both enabling and empowering (Dunst et al., 1988).

To construct programs that empower the individuals being treated, interventionists can be guided by the following three beliefs, as espoused by Dunst et al. (1988):

- People are already competent or capable of becoming competent.
- Failure to display competence does not result from deficits, but rather from the failure of a social system to create opportunities for competencies to be displayed (enabling experiences).
- To acquire a sense of control, the client must attribute behavior change to his or her own actions.

Implementing these concepts requires a shift and expansion in the traditional roles mental health professionals play in their interactions with children and families and in the ways in which these roles are performed. Dunst, Trivette and Deal's (1988) research has shown that recipients of help become effectively empowered only when they assume a high degree of responsibility for change.

Mental health professionals who work with families often overlook what may be the most effective resource—the family itself. Families usually have various unique strengths—perhaps a revered relative or a strong tradition—that can be worked into an intervention program to help meet a family member's needs. Interventionists can often benefit a family best by bolstering the family's ability to identify and utilize their own resources. This is a crucial component of planning for the time when the intervention ends. Help is most likely to have long-term benefits if the help-giver promotes the help-seeker's acquisition of effective behaviors that decrease the need for help. In other words, a primary goal is for the client to become more capable, competent, and independent. This goal, then, is the cornerstone of beneficial help-giving and help-seeking exchanges (Dunst et al., 1988).

In summary, the ecological viewpoint stresses the importance of involving individuals in shaping their environments in ways that are most useful to them. The goal is for the individuals to take ownership of their lives and to take some responsibility for solving their own problems. This is done by coupling the intervention with the environment in such a way that the program has credibility and authenticity in the eyes of those it affects (Trickett & Schmid, 1993).

Managed Care

Managed care has become the watchword in the 1990s for all health care. Take, for example, the growing interest in capitation systems in mental health care. McGovern and his colleagues (1990) have predicted a shift in psychotherapeutic practice with seriously mentally ill clients:

> Psychotherapy, in particular, will need to be attentive to the social network of the patient and, probably, be more invested in enlisting the involvement of naturally occurring supports (or contaminants) in the treatment process. This involvement could potentially result in less consumption of treatment re-

sources through the psychoeducational training of the family or social network, both of which are presumably cost-free service providers (p. 301).

Such a trend is not yet discernible. In fact, the provider manual of one of the largest managed care mental health organizations in the United States specifically lists "environmental ecology interventions" as an unreimbursed service.

Certainly the market forces now favor the inclusion of environmental interventions, but they have not been proven to be cost-effective. Mostly this is because such therapeutic approaches are relatively unknown or misunderstood by the mental health establishment, especially the private sector. But as noted in this chapter, there are significant populations which have demonstrated resistance to traditional mental health interventions. Historically, the public sector has served these populations. Now, as managed care organizations become increasingly responsible for entire populations, and paid on a capitated basis, there will be strong incentives to find cost-effective mental health interventions for clients who do not respond to traditional treatment methods. This circumstance will present an opportunity for environmental interventions, which have historically been judged as secondary to and less worthy than "psychotherapy," to be given a fair evaluation. And as argued in this book, environmental approaches may offer solutions both as supplements to traditional therapy and, with some clients, as the principal intervention.

4
Developing Ecological Consciousness

Chapter Preview
- Describes the difficulty traditionally trained practitioners may have thinking ecologically
- Presents 11 exercises to challenge readers to think ecologically

The attitude of mental health professionals stands as one of the greatest obstacles to implementing environmental approaches in interventions. Practitioners must be re-educated as to what is appropriate and what is effective in changing people's behavior. Unfortunately, most currently operating professional training programs—even those at the finest universities—are steeped in extremely traditional approaches to mental health service delivery. Graduates of these programs ordinarily receive little or no training in the range of environmental interventions consistent with ecological theory. This is analogous to a musical performer with an extremely limited repertoire—able to please a few people all of the time, but leaving the vast majority feeling unsatisfied. Mental health professionals must be prepared to "play to the masses."

Part of the reason for the lopsided curriculum is that training people to think ecologically is far more difficult than training them in traditional psychological assessment. Taking an environmental viewpoint requires a broader perspective—one that encompasses an array of factors external to the family. With an ecological perspective, because the problem is not viewed as residing within the child, the clinician must venture into and understand a vast environment of intervening and interwoven variables. The more factors that influence the child's behavior, the more difficult this is.

Even when professionals venture to provide individualized care, they are often limited by their ingrained focus on program components. Changing the focus of the service system to an individualized approach requires more than hard work and good intentions—it requires a complete paradigm shift (Olson, Whitbeck, & Robinson, cited in Katz-Leavy et al., 1992). To facilitate this necessary paradigm shift, the training of mental health professionals should emphasize the role of the child's social system in bringing about worthwhile change.

Friedman (1993) has outlined an academic curriculum geared toward producing broadly trained clinicians. This curriculum would train practitioners to understand the whole child, not just as an individual, but also as a participant in family, neighborhood, school, and community settings. Friedman also advocates providing mental health trainees with practical experience in diverse community settings. This real-world involvement should help trainees develop a flexible model for the interpretation of children's changing needs throughout childhood. Henggeler is another who has developed a comprehensive, "multisystemic" training program for child mental health professionals that is built on these ecological principles (Family Services Research Center, 1995).

This chapter presents a series of exercises designed to engage you, the reader, in ecological thinking. Be forewarned that thinking this way does not come naturally for some people. However, everyone—and clinicians in particular—can benefit from intergrating ecological consciousness into his or her view of the world of behavior.

Many factors in our lives conspire to restrict and shape how we view behavior (Leff, 1978). Any efforts to cultivate a more open-minded view are worthwhile. These exercises should help you become more sensitive to the effects of environments on people's behavior. You will be asked to rethink the ways in which you view children and families as you interact with them in helping relationships. These exercises are a modest first step in creating a fundamental paradigm shift, enabling you to perceive and understand events in a different way. Clinicians who develop creative ecological thinking skills will be better able to customize appropriate, effective interventions for their clients.

Exercise 1: Observer Attribution Bias

Is an individual's behavior ultimately caused by internal or external factors? In other words, to what do we attribute one's behavior? This is the central question addressed by attribution theory in the field of social psychology. Internal, or dispositional, factors include the personality traits, desires, and other dispositions that generally characterize a person. External, or situational, factors are the people and things involved in a specific situation that may cause a person to behave in a particular way. Being aware of external factors essentially involves taking the environmental view of things.

"Attribution" is the clinical term that refers to one's perception of the cause of an individual's behavior. One element that affects attribution is the amount of information the observer has about the situational factors surrounding a behavior. An observer who witnesses only an individual's behavior does not have much data about the situational factors affecting the individual. In such a case, when situational factors are either hidden or unknown, an observer is normally more inclined to make dispositional attributions about the individual's behavior. This inclination of the observer to overestimate the role of dispositional factors in influencing an individual's behavior is known as *observer attribution bias.*

In one study, Harari and Hosey (1981) found that everyone they studied, including clinicians, displayed a greater observer attribution bias when presented with a clinical scenario than when presented with a nonclinical one. It has been suggested that clinicians are particularly susceptible to this bias because of their "person-focused" training and professional norms (Jones & Nisbett, 1971). They are conditioned to look first to the individual as the source of problems, although this is not always therapeutically warranted.

Imagine that you are walking down the street and witness the following scene:

> A man in his early 20s (whom you don't know) stands at an open second-story window of a home. He unzips his pants and urinates out the window.

What are your first impressions? What is causing this man's behavior? Do you consider the behavior pathological? Do you attribute the young man's behavior to something about him? If so, what?

Now, step back from the situation. Did your answers express the observer attribution bias? That is, did you judge the young man's behavior based on assumed internal, personality factors? If so, consider some of the situational (environmental) factors that might have influenced the man to behave in such a manner. Try to generate a list of at least ten external factors that could have contributed to the observed behavior. Assuming that all behaviors have both internal and external factors, which type of factors do you think were more prominent in this case?

Exercise 2: Ecological vs. Linear Thinking*

Consider the way two drivers, one a linear thinker and one an ecological thinker, might approach the experience of being caught in a traffic jam. The linear thinker (who thinks in a straight, circumscribed fashion) would perhaps attribute the congestion to too many cars using too narrow a road. Widening the road might seem to be the logical solution in the linear-thinking person's view. Once the road was widened and the traffic congestion continued, the logical linear sequence would be to build additional roads—and more parking places and gas stations. If the city continued to grow, and businesses and services became harder still to reach, more and bigger roads would be necessary, of course. Meanwhile, as all the construction caused bigger and more frequent traffic jams, the linear thinker would probably keep a bottle of tranquilizers handy to help cope with the stress.

Now let's look in on the ecological thinker, just a few cars back. This person would probably see the traffic jam as only one symptom of a

---

* Adapted from Leff (1978).

malfunctioning transportation system. The "more" and "bigger" solutions that were popular with the linear thinker would not appeal to this ecological thinker. She or he would foresee the negative long-term consequences of such short-sighted actions: urban sprawl, diminishing public transportation, increased pollution, more watershed problems, and on and on. The ecological viewpoint would involve searching for broader explanations and solutions. The transportation system would be viewed as one strand in the social matrix. The ecological thinker might wonder: When are the roads most congested? Could local businesses perhaps stagger their work schedules? What incentives could be used to encourage the use of public transportation or to increase the average number of riders per car? Is a relatively low cost of fuel encouraging excessive vehicle use? Could speed limit modification/enforcement help manage the flow of traffic?

This example of the linear and ecological approaches to a particular situation is intended to give you a feeling for the differences between these two ways of thinking about people–environment relations. It is also meaningful to ponder how such different ways of thinking arise, in part, as a function of one's professional training. A person's way of thinking is in large part acquired—it is a habit. As such, it is open to modification. Ecological thinking can be nurtured by focusing on the critical elements of people-environment systems. The hallmarks of ecological thinking are the consideration of (1) the contexts of particular circumstances, (2) the interrelationships among all the variables in an environment, and (3) the long-term effects as well as the immediate ramifications of introducing a change into a people–environment system.

Exercise 3: Relativity of Disturbance

In traditional mental health models, behaviors are often broadly categorized as either normal or abnormal. For example, hearing voices is one of the behaviors typically classified as abnormal. Rosenhan (cited in Willems, 1977) illustrated this point when he asked eight entirely sane people to apply for admission to mental hospitals. One alleged reason for the applications was hallucinatory auditory sensations—all the eight subjects claimed to hear voices. In all but one of the cases, schizophrenia was diagnosed by psychiatrists, and seven "patients" gained entry to mental hospitals. In this study, clinicians simply listened as the individuals described their symptoms, a standard technique.

In an ecological view of the world, however, behaviors are evaluated within the context of their environmental circumstances. From this perspective, behavior is always relative. For example, talking to oneself while in a group of people might be considered "disturbed" behavior, whereas talking to oneself while walking alone might not be (Paul & Epanchin, 1982). Using Figure 4-1, think of circumstances or environments in which the example behaviors would be considered "disturbed" and other equally possible situations in which they would be considered normal.

Exercise 4: Facilitative Environments*

One quality of a good environment is that it makes a person feel supported for the activities performed there. When a person identifies a good "working" environment, he or she usually seeks to use it and enjoy

* Adapted from Farbstein and Kantrowitz (1978).

Figure 4-1: Think of a Situation . . .

- When would screaming loudly in public be considered normal?
- When would it be considered disturbed?

- When would rocking back and forth be considered normal?
- When would it be considered disturbed?

- When would laughing be considered normal?
- When would it be considered disturbed?

- When would poor hygiene be considered normal?
- When would it be considered disturbed?

it again and again. Sometimes, people don't consciously recognize that an environment provides a good fit, but they generally realize that time spent there is enjoyable and that tasks performed there are accomplished easily.

Different people often have widely divergent opinions about what makes a good environment. Some people prefer to have other people around, whereas others prefer more secluded environments. Some people appreciate and prefer the convenience of living in a city, while others are turned off by all the hustle and bustle.

Think about all the environments you spent time in during the past week. Which ones do you remember as places where your activities were supported or enhanced? Select one environment that worked well for you—an environment where you felt comfortable, one that you found easy to use and in which you enjoyed spending time. Now close your eyes for 5 minutes and go back to that environment in your thoughts. Picture yourself standing quietly in that environment, and compare the activities of other people and their use of the environment with your own. How do you feel? Does anything in that environment impinge on you and make you feel uncomfortable or ineffective? If so, what?

Compare your feelings and experiences in this good environment with those in another environment. Can an environment make you feel good and still work poorly for you? In other words, is it possible to feel good in an environment in which your activities are not supported or enhanced? Alternatively, can an environment work well for you and yet not make you feel good?

People spend time in a wide variety of environments, choosing them, modifying them, and adapting to them. Some environments can make people feel uncomfortable. Many times this occurs because the environments are not suitable for the activities the people attempt to perform in them. Some environments, however, feel right to people, enhance their activities, and enrich their lives. Such environments are called *facilitative environments*. Mental health professionals commonly make assumptions about which environments are facilitative for their clients. How well these environments actually work for the clients depends, in part, on the accuracy of the assumptions made.

Spend 5 minutes thinking about all the positive things an environment might have to offer one of your clients. Focus on a place that might work well for a child with a particular problem.

Exercise 5: Behavior Settings and the Behaviors They Encourage

Make a list of several settings where you choose to spend a portion of your time. Now analyze these settings to see if you can identify the situational properties (environmental factors) that predispose you to act or feel a certain way. For example, when you are stressed out, you might take walks on a quiet nearby beach at the end of the day. Try to determine what it is about the beach that has a calming, relaxing effect on you. Perhaps at times when you need to get some work done over a weekend, you find it difficult to do the work at home, but going to the local college library enables you to complete the work efficiently in a few hours. What is it about the library setting that enhances your productivity?

After you have identified several settings and the behaviors they encourage in your life, extend the list by analyzing several settings that you are less familiar with and try to determine the possible behaviors these settings might encourage for some people.

Exercise 6: The Eco-Map

A tool frequently used to assess the environmental elements and interconnections in a person's life is the eco-map. In this exercise, you will construct an eco-map of your life-space, photocopying and filling in the template on the next page, or, if you prefer, using a blank piece of paper.

To construct an eco-map, you draw a circle for each of the domains in your life-space. Some example domains are already identified on the template in Figure 4-2. The size of a circle should signify the relative number of people you interact with in that domain, and the distance between the circles should indicate how close the relationships are. In each domain, write the names of the people you are involved with.

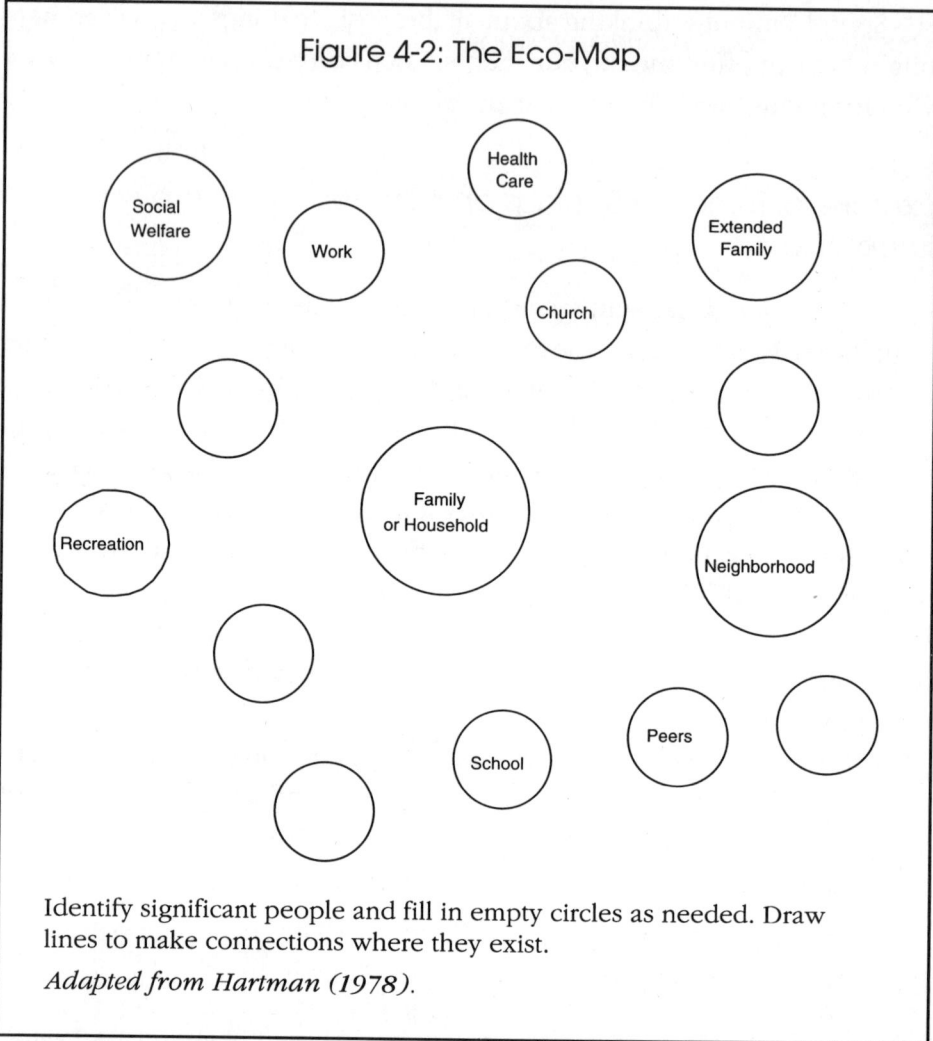

Identify significant people and fill in empty circles as needed. Draw lines to make connections where they exist.

Adapted from Hartman (1978).

Draw lines between the various circles to show interrelationships, and then draw arrows along the lines to signify the flow of involvement. If the relationship is predominantly stressful, draw a zig-zag line; draw straight lines for mostly supportive relationships. A completed eco-map should succinctly show what supports you enjoy, the place you and your family occupy in the environment, and the boundary between the family and the environment.

Exercise 7: Personal Networking Survey

Make a photocopy of the Personal Network table in Figure 4-3 (p. 56). In the first column, list the first names of the people (relatives, friends, neighbors, co-workers, etc.) you can rely on to help you and your family in a time of need. In the subsequent columns, add the following information for each person:

1. What is the relationship of the person to you?
2. How long have you known the person, and how frequently do you see each other?
3. What type of assistance does or could the person offer? Include any concerns or emotional needs this person can help you with.
4. How willing is the person to help you, and how helpful would the assistance be?
5. Have you ever done anything to help the person?
6. How much trouble is it for you to use this person? List specific obstacles to obtaining the person's help.

Exercise 8: Informal Social Supports

Robert Fulghum, in his book *All I Really Need to Know I Learned in Kindergarten* (1988), tells a delightful story about his barber. Fulghum telephoned his barber to make his usual appointment. To his dismay, he discovered that his barber had left to pursue a career in building maintenance. Fulghum compares the experience to that of a death in the family. Each month or so, Fulghum had argued, joked, and discussed important world events with his barber. While they never saw each other outside the barbershop, Fulghum came to know much about the barber's life, and the barber about his. The relationship, though not that of an intimate friend, had become an important fixture in his life—perhaps even more, he says, than if they had been next-door neighbors. Fulghum notes that without realizing it, we fill important places in each other's lives: a minister, a guy at the corner grocery store, the mechanic at a local garage, the family doctor, teachers, neighbors, co-workers, etc. Ac-

Figure 4-3: The Personal Network

First Name	Relationship to You	Length of Relationship/ Frequency of Contact	Type of Help	Willingness to Help/How Helpful	Are You Helpful to This Person?	Difficulties Using This Person for Help
1						
2						
3						
4						
5						
6						
7						
8						
9						
10						

cording to Fulghum, these are "good people, who are always 'there,' who can be relied upon in small, important ways. People who teach us, bless us, encourage us, support us, uplift us in the dailiness of life" (1988, p. 80).

It is easy to identify the principal supportive people in our lives. However, think about Fulghum's experience with his barber and see if you can identify some less obvious, but important, supportive people in your life. Where and how often do you see each person? What makes the relationship supportive? Can you think of a time when such a person disappeared from your support system? How did it affect you? Try to make a list of these "good people" in your life.

Exercise 9: Alternative Care Resources in the Community

Hollister, Edgerton, and Hunter (1985) have developed a useful exercise to facilitate a broad survey of community resources to assist clients. First, identify all the traditional resources you can easily identify—those which are obvious. Next, consider the array of less-obvious resources that could be tapped to assist clients. Finally, identify resources that you may have to help establish. Take a look at the generic resources listed below, and then see if you can make a comprehensive list for your own community. Be sure to note the *specific* resource on your own list. For example, instead of "helping neighbor," state the person's name. Likewise, if several social service agencies are resources, list the name of each.

Resources We Have Now
- private and public schools
- public welfare agencies
- specialty programs in alcohol and drug abuse
- private social service agencies
- general hospitals
- nursing homes
- crisis/emergency services
- mental health center
- courts

- others

  Potential Collaborations Available
- family
- friends and neighbors
- natural helpers in the community
- volunteer associations
- social clubs
- clergy
- police
- physicians
- local merchants
- others

  Resources We Need to Set Up
- self-help groups
- recreation
- club leaders
- vocational
- others

Exercise 10: Behavior Through Six Lenses

This exercise is designed to give you the experience of evaluating a child with special needs from six different perspectives—through six different lenses, so to speak. Each viewpoint has some relevance and contributes to the understanding of the child's behavior. Begin by reading this short vignette:

> Tommy is a third-grader in a public school. Ever since the first grade he has been identified as a child with severe behavior problems. Besides having difficulty staying on task, Tommy often refuses to participate in classroom activities and to do assigned school work. He flaunts the fact that his mother says he doesn't have to do it. He bullies the other children, fighting them during recess, verbally teasing other boys, and sometimes destroying others' work.

Although Tommy is of average intelligence, he can read only at a first-grade level. His math skills, however, are good. He is very talented in art and spends much of the day drawing in class. He also has demonstrated some athletic talent.

The major difficulty with Tommy is his acting-out behavior. He will not tolerate pressure of any kind in the class, and when the teacher demands that he participate in an assignment, he often flies into a rage. In such rages, he may strike out or kick and may also shout obscenities.

His teacher is, quite understandably, at the end of her rope. She spends much of her time in Tommy's corner of the classroom trying to keep him from hurting others. She and the principal have begun a disciplinary program in which Tommy's participation in recess is contingent upon his good behavior. So far, this effort has been ineffective in changing the unacceptable behavior.

Tommy has made some slow progress in one-to-one tutoring sessions, but he resists being followed around the school by a teacher's aide. His mother has been very uncooperative with the school. She refuses to consider placing him in another class or setting where his behavioral problems might be more adequately addressed. Tommy has little desire to do well in school.

Tommy's home life doesn't help. His father is in prison, and his mother receives welfare. He has three older brothers, and his teenage sister, who is pregnant, has left home and moved in with an aunt. Tommy spends most of his time at home unsupervised.

According to the six major models of behavior listed below, where do you think Tommy's disturbance lies? For each model, jot a few notes regarding the salient issues that the model contributes to understanding Tommy's behavior. In your view, which model contributes the most to an understanding of this case? Which contributes the least? Which model offers possibilities for the most effective intervention?

- Biological (physical issues)
- Psychodynamic (intrapsychic issues)
- Behavioral (learning contingencies)
- Cognitive (cognitions)
- Family Systems (intrafamilial interactions)
- Environmental Ecology (physical/social/institutional environments)

Exercise 11: Growing Up in Normal Environments

Find a comfortable place to sit. Close your eyes and relax. In your mind's eye, take a trip back into your childhood. Some avenues for you to explore are given here, but you are free to go where your memories take you.

Pick a time in your life of which you still have vivid memories: perhaps when you were a child, around age 9 or 10, or when you were a teenager, around age 14 or 15. Begin by identifying your life space—the principal areas where you carried out your life. Typically, these include your family, neighborhood, and school; there may be other areas such as church life or your parent's place of work, or even your own place of work. Take a few minutes to revisit each of these life spaces, to reacquaint yourself with your life when you were young.

Now that you have revisited the geography of your childhood, think about some specific places—places that made you feel competent, places where you felt good about yourself. Pick one. What about the place was so positive in your life? Did you learn something there? Were you challenged? Were you free from stress there?

Now in your mind's eye, go to a place that was not so positive for you. Try to identify what made it a place where you did not feel good about yourself.

Children learn to be healthy, fully functioning human beings by interacting meaningfully with diverse people in natural environments. Examples of healthy developmental environments include: families in which all family members sit down to eat dinner and share the activities of the day; neighborhoods where a child shovels snow from a neighbor's driveway for extra money and builds a tree fort with friends on a vacant lot; schools where a child learns among diverse peers and is encouraged to "hustle" by a coach in after-school volleyball; communities where a child works on a building project for the Boys Club and takes music lessons from a retired musician or local college student; church groups in which a youth eats Sunday dinner with a friendly group of peers who discuss their frustrations about teachers at school; a hospital volunteer program or a job at a local ice cream parlor in which a child learns that certain social graces come first, even when someone is discourteous to you.

This is how competent children learn to function well. If a child has trouble functioning in these natural environments, what then? Is it logical to totally abandon these powerfully competence-building environments and place the child in more sterile, controlled surroundings? Instead, for a child who has trouble negotiating her natural environments, all the necessary supports should be put in place *in these environments* to enable the child to survive there and begin to take advantage of the competence-building opportunities these environments offer.

Burchard and his colleagues (1993) defined the intervention strategy of "normalization" as the support of a lifestyle as similar as possible to that of the child's peers. In other words, the services used and the lifestyle promoted should be as culturally, ethnically, and age-appropriate as possible. Ultimately, belief in the viability of treatment in a closed setting (e.g., a group home) is based on the assumption that the problem is "in" the person rather than "in" the interaction and interdependence of the person and his or her life-space environments. Clinical environmental intervention, on the other hand, is centered on the belief that an individual's best hope for treatment and long-term effects is in receiving support in the real context of his or her life. Individuals with mental health problems must work through their issues while living in and dealing with their real, everyday environments (Burchard & Clarke, 1990).

Conclusion

Hopefully, the foregoing ecological exercises have helped infuse greater meaning into what is meant by ecological or environmental thinking.

With the groundwork laid for the model, the chapters that follow explicate some specific principles for translating ecological theory into practice, including assessment approaches and intervention domains.

5 The Environmental Status Exam for Intervention Planning

Chapter Preview
- Describes characteristics of the Environmental Status Exam (ESE)
- Describes the use of the "thick description" of children's lifestyles
- Identifies the time-use pattern as one of the principal ways of evaluating children
- Outlines hallmarks of the ESE
- Gives examples of an ESE and of an Environmental Support Plan (ESP)

Mental health assessment, as it is typically practiced, often has these characteristics:

- It is a discrete phase that is completed prior to intervention.
- It requires considerable effort and energy, and it usually leads to few intervention alternatives.
- It commonly makes use of arcane psychological methods.
- The principal goal is to establish an accurate diagnosis.
- It is predominantly office-based. This, coupled with the use of obscure psychological tests, tends to distance the client from the helper and the help being given.

The Environmental Status Exam, on the other hand, has these characteristics:

- It is an exploratory process; "diagnosis" is not seen as a useful concept.
- It is ongoing; it becomes directly linked to the intervention.
- It uses practical tools that do not require psychological sophistication to complete.
- It usually requires moving into the child's natural environment to get a proper perspective on what the problems and solutions might be.

A fundamental premise of the ecological viewpoint is that an individual and his or her environment interact in such a way that each shapes and influences the other toward adaptive balance. This perspective has broad implications for intervention efforts. Rather than focusing on the person and asking, "Now, what seems to be the problem here?" the interventionist views the entire life realm of the person and asks, instead, "What is not working here? Where is there a lack of fit that causes stress and behavioral maladaptation in the person?" The point of concern becomes how interrelated sets of personal, socioenvironmental, and non-socioenvironmental factors join together to create the problem. In performing an assessment, then, a clinician seeks to track the changing unit of analysis, continually analyzing person-related and environment-related characteristics in interaction (Tracy & McDonell, 1991). Moos (1976) refers to this assessment of a person's fit with his or her settings—an individual's "ecological niche," so to speak—as an Environmental Status Exam, or ESE.

In conducting an ESE, it is important to find out what the child does, with whom, and where. The objective is to acquire an in-depth description of the daily contexts that make up the child's life. Knowledge of the various factors involved in each of the environments helps the interventionist construct meaningful environmental interventions with families in a number of ways. Based on the ESE, appropriate actions can be planned to enhance the quantity and/or quality of the family's environmental resources. For example, it might be helpful to augment a family's social network—perhaps by providing volunteers, such as parent aides—to support the family's change efforts. Or perhaps a member of the family could benefit from experiencing more meaningful social connections outside the family. A "Big Brother" for a school-aged child, an exercise class for a young mother, or a support group for parents of a substance-abusing adolescent might help in this respect (Tracy & McDonell, 1991).

Gump (1984) reports an experience that helped him realize more clearly how the theory and methods of the ecological viewpoint are relevant to the evaluation of a client. A young female outpatient was assessed by clinicians from a number of different orientations. Each clinician used a particular assessment tool—psychiatric interview, Rorschach test, Thematic Apperception Test, etc. Gump's strategy was simply to learn about the woman's behavior over a typical weekend. Instead of attempting to discover her personality traits, he wanted to focus on her activities, which she described to him in detail. When all the evaluation results were in, Gump concluded that the woman's behavior could be explained much more thoroughly with the ecological inquiry added to the traditional techniques than with those techniques alone forming the sole basis of the assessment. Gump summarized his findings well in suggesting that the individual is not "sick" so much as his or her *lifestyle* is "sick."

Also promoting ecological inquiry, Csikszentmihalyi and Larson (1984) suggest that the treatment of various disorders requires the knowledge gained from a "thick description" of an individual's daily life. Looking "thickly" simply means not stopping with a quick appraisal of what may, on the surface of things, seem to be the problem. Instead, all the different levels of experience must be investigated. Every underlying environmental structure merits observation and consideration, because each fills an important place in the individual's life-space. Clearly, more "thick" knowledge is needed about the daily scenarios that make up the lives of depressed, anxious, conduct-disordered, or drug-dependent teenagers. How do they spend their free time? How do the activities and events in their lives affect their experiential states? What inhibits them from participating in the types of leisure activities that play such constructive roles in the lives of other teens?

The pattern of time use is one of the most revealing characteristics of a person or a group. In fact, in trying to understand the differences between people, the most important thing to find out could be how they spend their time. Given approximately 112 waking hours each week (16 or so per day), each of us selects, either actively or passively, a unique sequence of scenarios to fill those hours, and the choices we make help determine what our lives are like. The choices made are especially crucial for youngsters, because childhood patterns of time use help set the future course of one's life (Csikszentmihalyi & Larson, 1984).

So, what methods do interventionists have at their disposal to document clients' patterns of time use? In one study, Csikszentmihalyi and Larson (1984) asked a group of youngsters to carry electronic pagers and sheets of self-report forms. Over the course of a week, the youngsters were beeped at 40 randomly chosen moments, and each time the beeper went off they were asked to complete a report form, answering such questions as: Where are you? What is the main thing you're doing? What skills/challenges are involved in the activity? Who are you with? As you were beeped, did you wish you were doing something else? What were you thinking about? How would you describe your mood? Your energy level?

Of course, retrospective interviews of the type mentioned in the Gump study are options, but not everyone has a totally reliable memory, and certain important occurrences may be subconsciously repressed. A simpler, more traditional way to gather data about a person's daily life is with a time diary. In this method, at a predetermined point during every waking hour of the day (for instance, on the half hour), the client simply jots down a diary entry that addresses these questions:

- What are you doing?
- Who is present?
- Where are you?
- What is your affective state?

The beeper time sampling method noted above was used to identify 13 principal domains of a child's pattern of time use (Larson & Richards, 1989):

- Classwork
- Homework
- Personal Maintenance (eating, grooming)
- Household Maintenance (chores)
- Talking/Friends
- Media
- Sports
- Community Activities
- Employment
- Sleeping
- Hobby
- Extracurricular at School
- Church/Synagogue

Examining these domains and how they shape children's experiences is a major goal of the Environmental Status Exam. An analysis of a child's pattern of time use presents a fairly clear and consistent picture of the life environment of the child (Csikszentmihalyi & Larson, 1984).

The following sections introduce features that characterize the Environmental Status Exam. Other assessment tools may incorporate some of the concepts presented here, but they all come together in the ESE.

Assessment in the Natural Environment: In-Home Evaluation

The implications of specific environmental factors in the development of human problems can be more fully appreciated by clinicians who experience direct exposure to their clients' home environments. Direct observation of the physical characteristics of the home and of family members interacting with each other as they confront environmental stressors can be invaluable to the assessment and intervention efforts. What's more, stepping into a client's home environment is often the only way to engage all family members—particularly those who are reluctant to get involved—in the intervention program. In a client's home, the clinician is in a unique position to assess person-environment interactions, and to understand the role of social and physical factors in the development and amelioration of family problems (Tracy & McDonell, 1991). In short, an ESE can be more comprehensive, accurate, and useful when it includes firsthand information from the client's home setting. Home visits also are invaluable in helping clinicians understand the realities of life for families from different cultural backgrounds.

In addition to enhancing information gathering, in-home evaluations can provide a psychological boost to the client and the family in a number of ways. By conveying the clinician's interest in the client's family members and their living situation, home visits can foster a more cooperative, collaborative relationship with the client. Experiencing real-life events directly with the family can be a bonding experience. By going into the home of a client, a clinician demonstrates that the family really is in control of what takes place. Furthermore, people usually feel more comfortable on their own turf, and they usually relay information much more reliably when they are relaxed (Tracy & McDonell, 1991).

Identification of Prior Intervention Efforts

Another important element of the ESE is the identification and assessment of prior intervention efforts. Because ecological evaluation involves analyzing contextual factors, knowledge of past events (including earlier intervention efforts) can enhance the understanding of present circumstances. A convenient tool for gathering this type of information and presenting it in a visually meaningful way has been developed by Burchard and his colleagues (1993). They advocate constructing timelines that delineate a youth's history in five critical areas: behavior, events, education services, family services, and residential services. Stacking these five timelines together yields a composite picture of the child's past and makes it easy to review prior intervention efforts and to see interrelationships among the different categories. Figure 5-1 is an example of such a timeline snapshot of an 11-year-old named Benny.

The Interview as Environmentally Friendly Evaluation Instrument

Formal evaluation instruments are rarely used as part of an ESE because clients often have trouble relating to them, and this can have the ultimate effect of distancing the client from the worker (Maguire, 1991). ESEs are typically conducted through interviews. Some important guidelines for interviewing children and other family members include:

- Focus on the daily lifestyle of the family.

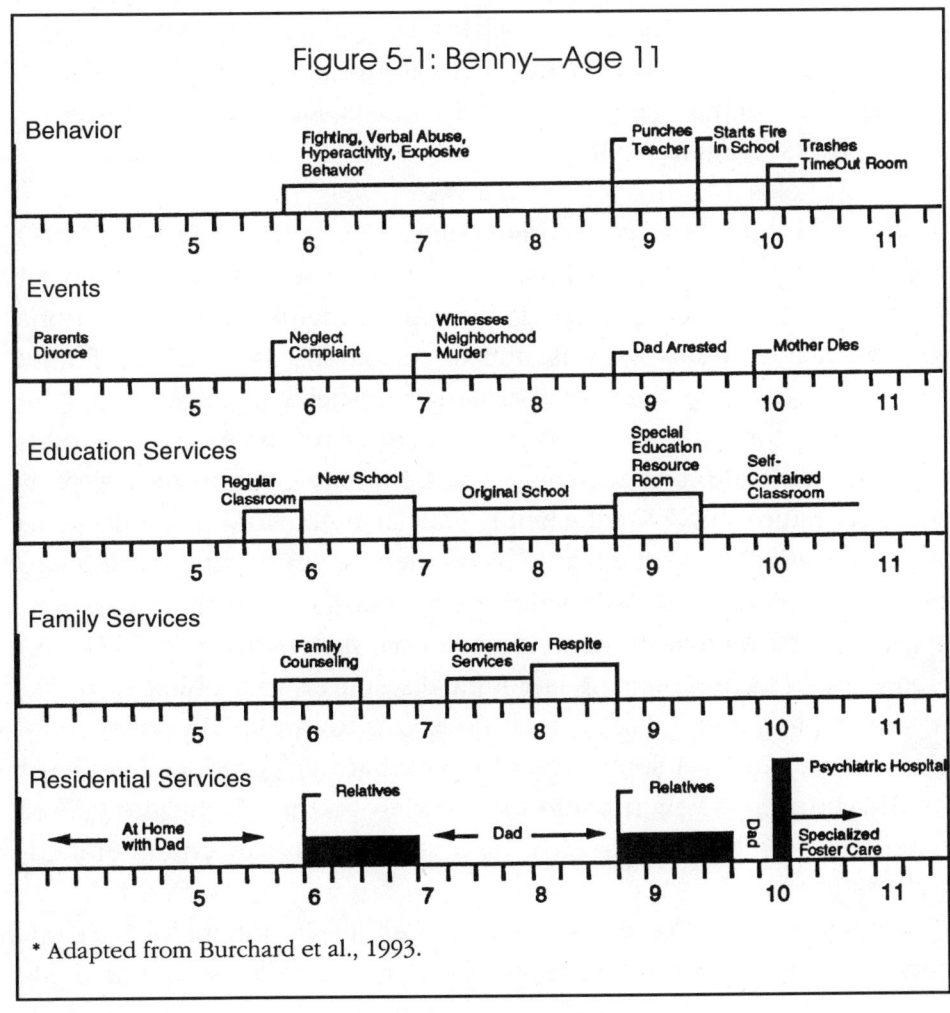

- Pay particular attention to people, places, and activities in the child's life.
- Identify those aspects of the physical and social environments that reflect strengths.
- Ask the family members to describe the ways in which they deal with daily routines.
- Ask the family about hobbies, interests, etc.
- Observe the physical environment.
- Ask about neighborhood involvement (interaction with neighbors).
- Ask about memberships in organizations such as religious or church groups, self-help groups, sororities or fraternal organizations, unions, ethnic clubs, social clubs, political groups or causes, sports or athletic teams, and parent groups or organizations. Also, seek to identify neighborhood hangouts such as bars or street corners (Maguire, 1991).

In addition to these general guidelines, Tracy and McDonell (1991) suggest using some of the following questions to assess a family's social support network: Does the family have meaningful social connections with other individuals, groups, and organizations? If so, are all family members involved or are some isolated from such exchanges? Does the family have adequate access to needed social resources, such as education, health care, and recreation? Is the family open to new experiences or relationships? Are the family's social interactions generally positive or negative? Does the family have adequate opportunities to share cultural, religious, and other values? Questions such as these can help pinpoint person-environment interrelational factors that should be explored either as problems or as potential solutions to problems.

Assembling a long list of stock questions for an ESE interview may be a daunting task for some. The eco-map that was introduced in Chapter 4 can be used to help structure an interview and enable the interviewer to gather information about environmental resources in a more unified, systematic manner.

Finally, in assessing settings as resources, it is important for the clinician to consider not only those settings that already exist, but also potential settings that, if created, might help resolve problems (Trickett & Schmid, 1993).

Diagnosis

The ecological orientation requires that diagnoses be interactive. To claim that a child is disturbed, or that a child has a disorder, isolates the disturbance within the domain of the individual. Saxe, Cross, and Silverman (1988) note that traditional diagnoses operate this way, ignoring important environmental covariants of children's mental health disorders. Echoing this theme, Burchard and Clarke (1990) note that even for youths with identical diagnoses, the fact that an individual's resources and challenges are highly idiosyncratic makes it impossible to treat each youth effectively with the same intervention program. Because clinicians planning environmental treatment services are individual-focused, traditional psychiatric diagnostic categories tend to be of little value to them.

To be meaningful, the perspective must be shifted away from a narrow focus on the individual to a broader view that encompasses the individual-in-the-setting. When the true location of disturbance—within the ecosystem—is acknowledged and understood, disturbances can be dealt with more efficiently and effectively. The term "ecosystemic deficit disorder" (EDD, for short) has been proposed as a catch-all diagnosis designed to address any situation in which there are deficits in the functioning of relationships in the systems and subsystems of family, school, and community (O'Callaghan, 1993).

Focus on Strengths

Any mental health evaluation of a child and the child's environment should focus on strengths. Furthermore, one of the aims of assessment and intervention should be to recognize and build upon the unique expertise that all parents bring to the child-rearing process. Everyone has some talents, and a positive focus on how a parent's natural abilities can be used to help solve family problems can be a strong motivating and enabling force.

Identification of Behavior Sequences

The ESE should help the interventionist identify key behavior sequences in the child's life, particularly those behaviors that lead up to the problem behavior(s) of concern. Again, the value of the ecological approach in addressing the context and interactive nature of behaviors is evident. It is usually much more important to understand the context of a behavior than to understand the behavior itself. The sequence of events that precede an undesirable behavior can give a picture of how and why the behavior occurs. With this understanding, the interventionist can design ways of disrupting the sequence and forestalling the behavior. This is similar to the concern of the behaviorist with the relationship of stimulus and consequent events to target behavior (Fine, 1992).

Person-Environment Fit

The appropriateness of behavior is relative. A behavior that is adaptive in one context may be maladaptive in another. This fact suggests that part of the ESE should be geared toward discovering how different contexts push and pull the child in different directions (Trickett & Schmid, 1993). Henggeler (1991) notes that one of the primary purposes of assessment is to understand how the child fits into his or her broader systemic context.

Ongoing Evaluation

During the first few months of community-based intervention, it is common for youths to continue to display the same behaviors they displayed previously. Behavior change usually occurs only after the youth has thoroughly tested the rules and attempted to disrupt the planned changes (Burchard et al., 1993). Clinicians who are performing an ESE must keep this in mind and be sure to continue the assessment for an extended period. This is less difficult with the ESE, which becomes interwoven with the intervention, than with other more traditional assessment tools, which are more self-contained.

Environmental Support Plan (ESP)

Ecological mental health diagnosis is unambiguous and intuitive. Rather than being classified according to traditional categories (as with DSM-IV), children are assessed by identifying the environmental supports they require to attain some reasonable level of behavior adjustment. Using the information gathered in the ESE to identify what supports are needed, the clinician should design an Environmental Support Plan (ESP). The ESP becomes the action plan for the intervention, providing a step-by-step guide for modifying the child's ecosystem so that it functions satisfactorily and supports the desired behavior modification.

The ESP should identify the processes and actions that are necessary to integrate persons, settings, and events into a cohesive intervention plan. How these various resources are combined depends on the particular context of the problem(s) being addressed (Trickett & Schmid, 1993). After the outline of the ESP is completed, principal ecosystem members meet to delineate for each step:

- Who will be responsible for getting the task done.
- Who will actually provide the service, if a service is required.
- By what date the service will be completed or the goal achieved.
- What, if anything, the service will cost.
- If it costs, where the money will come from.
- What criterion/criteria will be used to determine whether objectives have been met.
- What follow-up steps might be required.

Crisis Planning

It is unrealistic to think that any intervention will totally eliminate episodes of disruption for the youth being treated. Rather, it is assumed that disruptions will occasionally occur, always with the potential of creating a crisis situation for the youth, the family, and even the service system. A realistic objective for any intervention program is to help make disruptions and crises less frequent, shorter in duration, and less intensive (i.e., less alarming and less dangerous). Proper service planning allows for occasional setbacks and strives for gradual improvement. Interventionists should not let occasional crises discourage them into giving up on the youth or making radical changes in the program.

The best way to deal with episodic crises is to adopt a proactive approach—to "nip them in the bud" and not wait for them to develop. Nonetheless, an ESP should contain contingency plans for crisis situations, complete with short-term, back-up alternatives to the main strategies being used (Burchard et al., 1993). Often, all that is needed is the timely insertion of trained personnel to defuse or stabilize a crisis situation. Having predetermined contingency plans will make it highly unlikely that a child will ever have to be removed from his or her natural setting.

Case Analysis and Sample Environmental Support Plan

A sample of an Environmental Status Exam and a corresponding Environmental Support Plan are presented in the ensuing pages. The plan should result in the development of processes to integrate persons, settings, and events into an intervention plan. How resources are combined depends on the ecology of the particular context and the problem around which resources are mobilized (Trickett & Schmid, 1993).

Presenting Problem

Jason is a 10-year-old white male in the fourth grade at Washington Elementary School. His father is deceased, and Jason lives with his grandparents, who are having difficulty handling him. According to the grandparents, he was traumatized by the separation from his mother, whom he sees only infrequently. He exhibits both academic and behavioral problems. At home Jason acts immature and disobeys often. At school he often disrupts the class, and he has difficulty reading. Jason was referred to the Mental Health Center by Mrs. Heath, his classroom teacher.

Individual Analysis

Jason's teacher and his grandmother identify the following behaviors as being the most critical problems: 1) enuresis at home, 2) defiance of rules at home, 3) oppositional behavior at school, 4) failure to complete homework assignments, and 5) refusal to put forth effort in class.

The enuresis has been an almost nightly occurrence for the past year. The grandmother says that in addition to no longer doing his chores, Jason regularly disobeys her household rules. Disobedience usually occurs in the evenings, especially on weekends.

Jason's disruptive behavior at school occurs mostly in the mornings, which is also when his inattentiveness is most noticeable. A school psychologist recently performed a behavior sample and noted that Jason engaged in oppositional behavior 40% of the time. In the past week Jason failed to complete four out of five homework assignments. When he turns in completed homework, it is almost exclusively on Fridays.

When Jason wets the bed, his grandmother makes him hang up the sheets on the clothesline. Disobedience of family rules usually has no consequence. When he misbehaves in school, the teacher either ignores him or reprimands him. Oppositional behavior in the classroom occasionally leads to time-out or to corporal punishment (paddling) by the principal. When he fails to complete his homework, his recess privilege is sometimes withdrawn, but usually nothing happens. However, in the past Mrs. Heath has rewarded him with candy for completing his homework. The grandmother's reaction to bedwetting appears to be the only consistent behavioral consequence.

Throughout his childhood, Jason has received routine medical and dental care. He was prescribed Ritalin for a few months when he was in the first grade, and his grandmother fears it may have "done damage to his head." Presently, Jason is not taking any medication and has no apparent medical needs. Also, he has no known sensory deficits. His fine motor coordination is poor, but gross motor control is good. Jason's developmental history prior to the separation from his mother is uneventful. Since then, there has been only the immature behavior, which continues to the present.

Family Analysis

When Jason's mother was pregnant with him, his father abandoned them. The father is now deceased, and Jason's mother, who has worked as a waitress at a bar for the past 3½ years, has a severe drinking problem. Unable to supervise her children because of her evening work hours, she gave guardianship of Jason and his little brother Billy to her parents when Jason was 7 and Billy was 2 years old. She is rumored to be working as a prostitute in a larger city 40 miles away.

The grandparents, both in their mid-60s, are well-meaning caretakers, but they feel overwhelmed by Jason's problems. (Actually, the grandfather is rather uninvolved in Jason's upbringing and provides little in the way of a male role model.) Both the grandmother and the grandfather report that they and the two boys usually got along pretty well until about a year ago, when Jason became increasingly defiant.

The grandmother says she wishes she could "do right by" her grandchildren. She is at a loss to explain Jason's changed attitude and misbehavior. Although the household income is marginal, food, clothing, housing, and sanitation are all adequate. When asked why Jason's mother doesn't contribute any financial support, the grandmother says she thinks her daughter "spends all her earnings on her drug habit." The grandmother has "bad nerves," for which she takes Valium, and the grandfather has severe emphysema.

Jason's primary playmate is his younger brother. Jason doesn't belong to any peer organizations and doesn't participate in any sports or recreational programs. After school, he takes the bus home, where he is supervised by his grandparents. Overall, the family is quite isolated, both geographically and socially.

Peer Analysis

Jason has no friends at school, and he feels as if he has none in the home. Other than his brother, there simply are no children to associate with in his isolated home environment. Jason appears to have adequate social skills to make friends, but because he frequently bullies and fights children at school, no one wants to be his friend.

School Analysis

Jason's school performance is inconsistent overall, but fairly steady in some areas. He enjoys math, especially the math games Mrs. Heath does once a week, and his math performance (when he does the work) is at grade level or above. His reading skills, however, are at least two grade levels behind. He has trouble pronouncing some consonant sounds when he reads. A general lack of phonic word attack skills in reading has carried over into spelling difficulties.

Jason shows no deficiencies in his understanding and use of visual, auditory, and kinesthetic material, and screening tests indicate that he has no vision, hearing, or speech problems. He is able to maintain his attention for periods up to 30 minutes (average for his grade level) when he is motivated by the subject or when he is given special attention. Jason even has good memory skills. Still, he cannot do much of the age-appropriate work he is asked to do, and he copes in a classic way—by not trying. Consequently, he is unmotivated to do the work asked of him.

Mrs. Heath's classroom space is structured in the traditional manner for elementary schools: the students' desks are in rows facing the chalkboard, and the teacher's desk is in the front of the room facing the children. The daily class routine is fairly consistent, with reading, spelling, and science units in the mornings, followed after lunch by recess, math, and social studies periods.

Mrs. Heath incorporates a good amount of chalkboard-focused seatwork in her lessons, with intermittent periods of direct spoken instruction. Sometimes, the seatwork involves worksheets and textbooks, but practically always as individual assignments; there is virtually no group work. Washington Elementary does not track its students; that is, there is no grouping by ability—all students at a particular grade level receive and use the same materials.

When the students are busy working on worksheets, Mrs. Heath tends to remain at her desk. She occasionally reminds the students to raise their hands if they need individualized help from her, but they rarely do, and she rarely moves around the room. Students who have finished an assignment and have not yet received other work to do typically just sit and wait or recheck their work. Unless they are given permission to get up and move around the room, they are expected to remain in their seats.

During the instruction periods, Mrs. Heath gives her students plenty of opportunities for oral expression and other forms of active responding. To maintain order, she asks that they raise their hands to receive permission to speak. Most students are able to follow this guideline, but Jason seems to have trouble with it, often just blurting out his opinions.

Jason's peers view him as the class clown. They often egg him on to do something disruptive. The attention this brings from his classmates appears to outweigh any reprimands or punishments he receives from Mrs. Heath.

Mrs. Heath's implementation of behavior consequences is very inconsistent. She usually responds to student misbehavior with a verbal reprimand, and sometimes, especially in the period before recess, by threatening to withdraw the recess privilege. However, she does not always follow through with her threats. Occasionally, a child is sent out of the room to sit in the hallway. When a child performs well, Mrs. Heath showers him or her with lots of verbal praise. She has two Apple Macintosh computers in her classroom, but she has never attempted to use them for positive reinforcement (for example, by making them available for use by students who have completed an assignment). The computers are sometimes used during math period, and Mrs. Heath shows an instructional film about once a week.

Mrs. Heath receives help from one parent volunteer (a male), who comes in for two hours on Friday mornings. Students attend special art, music, and gym classes once a week, and Jason exhibits acceptable behavior in these classes. He is very athletic.

The school has a part-time guidance counselor but no reading specialist. A speech therapist visits the school one half-day a week. Jason has little contact with the principal, who tends to remain holed up in his office. On three occasions over the past 2 months, Mrs. Heath has sent Jason to the principal's office, where he was admonished and paddled.

Neighborhood/Community Analysis

Jason's grandparents have lived in their current house for 32 years. Jason has lived with them for almost 4 years now. Several other older farming couples live within a short drive, and Jason's grandparents enjoy occasional interaction with these neighbors. The area is quite depressed economically. One result of this is that there are no neighborhood recreational or social facilities, other than the church three miles down the road.

The grandparents are well-respected members of the church. Jason reluctantly attends the Sunday services with them and his brother. The pastor, a pleasant man in his early 40s, seems to be genuinely interested in helping the family, but he lacks confidence in his ability to counsel and intervene.

Other than regular trips into town on Saturdays to attend a few yard sales, the family members have little involvement in the community as a whole. They are presently using no community resources—no social welfare or legal agencies. The grandparents see the general practitioner in the county seat for their health problems. This is the same doctor who prescribed Ritalin for Jason 3 years ago.

Along with Mrs. Heath, and perhaps the school physical education teacher, the pastor appears to be the best community agent for intervening on Jason's behalf. The various community resources (i.e., the school, the church, and the medical community) have no prior experience of working together cooperatively on a social issue.

Family-Identified Goals

Primary goals are to decrease bedwetting episodes, decrease oppositional behavior at home and in the classroom, and increase the proportion of daily assignments completed. Jason is already quite capable of performing some of these desired behaviors. His grandmother reports that sometimes he goes several nights without wetting the bed. Also, since he demonstrates oppositional behavior 40% of the time he is in class, that means that 60% of the time he is not being disruptive. Although Jason completes his homework assignments only rarely, what is completed is usually done correctly. There seems to be a good solid basis for progressing toward achievement of the goals.

Ecological Integration

Jason's behavior is ordinarily appropriate at church, in the community (e.g., during shopping trips), and often in the afternoons at school and weekday evenings at home.

The interface between Jason's home setting and the situation with his mother appears to be extremely difficult for him. Jason's mother is very inconsistent with visits, and when she does visit, Jason is quite ambivalent. She does not send the boys birthday or Christmas presents. The grandfather is also uninvolved and is not a good role model. He usually waits in the car when the grandmother brings Jason to the Mental Health Center.

Jason seems unaware that his behavior fluctuates in different environments, although he does acknowledge that he feels relatively calm at school in the afternoons. He believes this calmness comes from his enjoyment of recess.

Jason appears to have a deficiency in attending-concentration skills. Both Mrs. Heath and the grandparents could benefit from some clarification of their expectations. At home, Jason must cease bedwetting and demonstrate compliance with some selected rules (e.g., in the house and washed up at dinnertime, in bed at bedtime, no sassing back). The grandparents have many expectations for Jason's compliance but do little to enforce the most significant rules.

At school, he must complete his assignments regularly and concentrate on his work while not disrupting the class. However, the morning period of instruction is very long, without a significant break between 8:30 and 12:00; modifying the classroom schedule could help to control some of Jason's disruptive behavior. Also, much of what is considered Jason's disruptive school behavior would present less of a problem if he were in a more open classroom arrangement.

Jason's two primary environments, the classroom and the home, are inadequate for meeting all of his developmental needs. He should be exposed to a wider variety of settings and a wider variety of people. Having a greater range of interactions would likely reduce some of the tensions in his two primary environments. The family pastor, a young priest, appears to be a potentially positive influence. In addition, the gym teacher/coach at school could be a beneficial influence.

The intervention will be targeted mainly at home rule consistency, participation in more varied settings, and classroom structure. The grandmother will be responsible for carrying out the behavioral programs at home to address the enuresis problem and the issue of consistent rule enforcement. The family pastor will be asked to help Jason get involved in some other activities and to provide some guidance and supervision. The school will modify Jason's classroom environment to enable him to receive more individualized instruction, and they will enlist a classroom volunteer to help monitor Jason's completion of assignments by using a daily report card. The school will also encourage Jason to get involved in after-school activities. A conference will be held that includes Jason, his grandparents, Mrs. Heath, the school counselor, the family pastor, and a mental health counselor, to inform these major players of the intervention being planned and their roles in it.

The school guidance counselor will act as the liaison between the school and home environments. She will contact both the grandmother and Mrs. Heath at the end of each marking period to help monitor Jason's progress throughout the upcoming year. Before placing Jason in next year's class, the counselor will consider the various teachers' styles to ensure the best fit possible. She will also spearhead an effort to get Jason involved in regular after-school activities, perhaps a club or an individualized exercise program with the physical education teacher. This expansion of involvement will give Jason more exposure to positive role models (both peer and adult) and should provide him with more opportunities to succeed.

Figure 5-2: Jason's Environmental Support Plan (ESP)

Child's Name	Jason White		Date	2/30
	Description of Problem			**Individual Level**
	Disruptive in school and has difficulty reading. Disobedient at home. Grandparents having difficulty handling him.		Anxiety: separation from mother Depression: none Anger/Aggression: aggressive with peers	Social skills: immature at home Intellectual/Academic: capable Medication: none Biological: bedwetting
	Child's/Family's Strengths			**Prior Interventions**
	Good ability in math. Maintains attention in one-on-one. Grandparents trying very hard to raise Jason; receptive to professional help.			Teacher used candy reward for completed homework. Paddling by principal. No remedial work in reading. Recess withdrawal. No history of out-of-home placement.
	Environmental Resources			**Crisis/Respite Plan**
Peers	No friends. Mostly plays with his brother. Needs opportunities to develop friendships.			Out-of-home placement is not presently a risk. Grandparents have mental health center 24-hour phone number and have been counseled how to use it. We also "practiced" using the 24-hour number late in the evening so they would feel comfortable using it if needed. Involvement in some structured activities after school will give grandparents some respite time.
School	Structured classroom. Need to modify schedule. No reading specialist. Gym teacher is a resource.			
Neighborhood	Family lives in isolated rural area. Family priest is potential resource.			
Community	Nearby community (10 mi.) has recreational program.			
Agencies	Not involved with any agencies.			

The Environmental Status Exam for Intervention Planning

Figure 5-2 (Continued)

Environmental Support Plan: Family Environment
Child's Name: Jason White

	Family Environment		Household Management
Parent-Child	Grandparents are very inconsistent with enforcing rules. Rules are not clear.	Eating/ Sleeping	Family eats breakfast and dinner together. Jason sometimes acts out at dinnertime because he wants to watch TV. Family has sleep routine, 10-6.
Siblings	Jason often fights with his younger brother.	TV/ Routines	Jason and his brother watch about 4 hrs. of TV every day. Grandparents watch none. Family drives to town to go to yard sales every Saturday a.m. and attends church Sunday a.m.
Marital	Grandfather is rather remote in all family relationships.	Homework/ Chores	Jason has no regular routine for completing homework at home. He is not responsible for any chores. He used to have to feed the chickens but was unreliable.
Kin	Jason's mother is involved very little with family and seldom visits.	Financial	Grandparents receive Social Security and have Medicare. Jason is eligible for Medicaid. Family finances are very tight. They do own their modest home.
Family Network	Grandparents have several neighbors whom they see daily.	Physical Environmt.	Home is well-kept, but no air conditioning makes the summer months uncomfortable.
Parent Employment	Grandparents are retired. Mother is drug addicted and works as a prostitute.	Transportation	The family owns an old car, but it appears reliable.
Supervision	Jason is well-supervised by grandparents at home and by teachers at school.	Medical Care	Grandfather sees a doctor regularly for emphysema. Jason has no medical problems.
Other	Grandfather's illness requires regular visits to the doctor.		

Figure 5-2 (Continued)

Environmental Support Plan: Goals & Implementation
Child's Name: Jason White

	Goal	Needed Resources	Implementation	Who is responsible for getting task done	Who actually provides service	By what date	Cost / Source of funds	How is it determined that objective is met	Follow-up
Family	1. Eliminate bedwetting	Structured behavioral program	Grandmother will use more structured approach to eliminate bedwetting	Dr. Jones	Grand-mother	3/10	none	2 dry weeks	Dr. Jones
	2. Increase compliance with rules	Key rules will be identified	Grandparents will be taught to use a rule-privilege program	Dr. Jones	Grand-mother	3/10	none	Regularly earns privileges	Dr. Jones
School	3. Resolve reading problem	Peer tutoring	School guidance counselor will set up peer tutoring	Mr. Willis	Jimmy Watts	3/15	none	Improved reading scores	Mr. Willis
	4. Increase on-task behavior	Add a.m. recess & math lab in p.m.	Jason will be allowed to use math lab if behavior is appropriate in a.m.	Ms. Smith	Ms. Smith	3/10	none	Earns math lab privileges	Ms. Smith
	5. Increase completion of assignments	Parent volunteer to monitor homework	Parent volunteer who is an admired adult will monitor homework	Ms. Smith	Mr. Dix	3/10	none	Daily homework completion	Ms. Smith
Peers/ Neigh-borhood	6. Augment social supports	4-H club, Boy Scouts	Jason will attend 4-H after school twice monthly. Grandmother will transport home. Family pastor will transport to twice-monthly scout meetings.	Father Caruso	4-H, Boy Scouts	3/15	$100 / Church	Attendance	Father Caruso
Agen-cies	7. Mental health counseling		Twice-monthly counseling with Dr. Jones	Dr. Jones	Dr. Jones	2/30	$80/wk. / Medicaid	Complete 10 sessions	Dr. Jones

Conclusion

Lee (1985) introduced a potentially useful concept with her "life-space structures." Beginning with the assumption that human beings are basically reinforcement-seeking creatures, she noted that certain patterns of living develop around a person's complex and primitive attempts to maximize rewards. In other words, people develop unique life-space patterns, or as Lee calls them, "characteristic ways of negotiating time, space, people, and activity in their day-to-day lives" (p. 624). These patterns help individuals cope with and structure their environments for the satisfaction of their needs and desires.

To achieve ecological balance, these environmental resources—time, space, people, and activity—must be accessible, usable, and pliable. The manipulation of these elements in a person's life is the core of clinical environmental intervention.

The importance of evaluating a child's—and family's—time use was discussed earlier in this chapter. The next three chapters are devoted to examining places (space), activities, and people as resources. The concept of time use remains an important factor in each of these other domains. The choices made in the selection and use of these three resources determine to a great extent how a person adapts to life's stresses.

6 Places As Resources

Chapter Preview
Describes 5 principal behavior settings and some of their influences on behavior:
- Home
- Neighborhood
- Workplace
- Church
- School

As mentioned earlier, the vast scope and interrelatedness of an individual's environment have been part of the reason why environmental intervention has been slow to catch on in the field of mental health. These factors tend to make analysis and discussion of the topic difficult. To further the current discussion, let us arbitrarily divide the environment into places, activities, and people.

The social environment has traditionally been a primary concern in the design of mental health interventions. Interpersonal and group dynamics have long been recognized as important factors in an individual's behavior patterns. In contrast, behavior settings (places)—the actual physical surroundings in which behavior occurs—have not been readily conceived and appreciated as intervention variables. This is unfortunate, because environmental settings can either constrain or enhance the possibilities for healthy behavior and development. Indeed, Belle (1989) suggests that parents and other socialization agents influence children's behavior more through their control of settings than through direct instruction.

This chapter explores five behavior settings where children typically spend an abundance of their time: home, neighborhood, workplace, church, and school. Although the central focus is on the places themselves, the activities carried out in those places and the people involved will, of course, enter the discussion. Broader community settings, such as those involving sports teams or clubs, will be discussed in Chapter 7, "Activities as Resources." And, while people are certainly influential factors in both places and activities, an in-depth consideration of people as environmental factors and intervention resources is reserved for Chapter 8.

Home Environment

Tracy and McDonell (1991) have identified what they call *background features* in the home environment. Background features are elements of the environment that do not draw immediate perceptual attention. Levels of noise and activity, as well as the size and number of rooms, are examples. Some background features can cause adverse behavioral effects; for example, high noise and activity levels often interfere with a child's ability to attend to a task. What's more, children growing up in noisy, action-packed environments commonly have difficulty acquiring auditory discrimination and visual search learning skills. The ratio of the number of people living in a home to the number of rooms in the home is another factor that affects mental health. Children in crowded living conditions, with little or no personal space, often feel powerless over environmental events.

Benjamin Spock, the esteemed pediatrician who wrote *Baby and Child Care*, notes that

> if the house is chaotic with a television blaring, people shouting, the telephone ringing and people running in and out, the child cannot do anything else but react in kind to the chaos. When the environment ... changes in the home, the tone is set

and the sense of calm and relaxation will be reflected in the child (Spock, 1994, p. 87).

Spock goes further to insist that medications and psychiatric treatment for many children simply permit children and their parents to ignore their bad habits.

Another major behavior-modifying factor in the home environment is an individual's privacy, or the lack thereof. Children who do not have rooms of their own or who live in multiple-unit dwellings are less likely to play in their own houses or yards or their friends' houses or yards (Medrich, Roizen, Rubin, & Buckley, 1982). Salzinger, Antrobus, and Hammer (1988) found that many children are accustomed to being moved from one room and/or bed to another in order to provide sleeping space for family guests. However, it is not known whether this disruption causes problems for some children.

Family Use of Time

Another vantage point from which to view the home environment is examining how families use time. In other words, what activities are planned and encouraged for the time that a child spends in the home? Of course, the discussion is drifting more toward activities here, but the focus is still on place—the home. The concern is with those activities that are predominantly identified with the home environment.

Mealtime. Bringing the entire family together around a central activity is a common tradition in family life. For example, the custom of families eating their meals at home together around a table and discussing the day's events and sharing ideas has been around for a long time. However, such family-focused dining has become the exception rather than the norm in America today. Many American families never eat together anymore; instead, individuals grab their meals as they come and go.

Many factors have conspired to create this situation. First, the family lunch disappeared when family members began eating at work or school. Then the family breakfast disappeared when everyone began leaving the home in the morning on different schedules. Now, with the hectic lifestyles of single parents or two working parents, only a small number of families sit down to dinner together every night, and many of those who do are grouped around a television set. According to a communications study at the University of Pennsylvania, 40% of families eat dinner in front of the television.

This haphazard meal situation is mostly a new American habit. In many countries, mealtime is still a special gathering time for families. In places where the food budget can take up to 40% of a family's income, eating is not taken for granted. Evening mealtime becomes a time for relaxation and family conversation, a time to discuss how the day went for everyone.

Of course, even in America there is a wide range of family dining habits. For example, African-American families in general are significantly less likely than white families to eat dinner together. Researchers report that African-American and low-income families have more permissive rules about after-school time schedules, dinnertime, and bedtime than do white and high-income families. Medrich and his colleagues (1982) found that children with no regular bedtime generally stayed up later than their peers on a stricter schedule.

Homework Time. Another home-centered activity with various behavioral implications is school homework. Not surprisingly, increased study time is associated with better academic performance. Parents who provide their children with the space, time, and encouragement to do their homework are taking steps that can help minimize in-school behavior problems. Providing the necessary homework support is not always easy, however. Larson and Kleiber (1993) report that children generally feel more unhappy, lethargic, and uninterested while doing homework than when they are performing other activities.

Parents can help make homework activities more successful and enjoyable. According to Larson and Kleiber (1993), a child's desire for companionship during homework time may reflect increasing internal motivation in the upper grade levels. Parents of these children would do well to encourage group study. Furthermore, Larson and Kleiber found that homework done with a parent or other family member present is associated with the highest attention levels and better performance.

Household Chore Time. Boys from dual-earner families who are highly involved in household tasks see themselves as more competent and rate their relationships with their parents more positively than do their peers who perform fewer chores around the house. With single-earner families, however, boys who are highly involved in housework see themselves as less competent than their peers who have fewer household chore responsibilities. While it is desirable for all children to have assigned chores, the amount of time and responsibility should be reasonable. For example, in some households, older siblings are expected to care for younger ones. Parents must monitor such responsibility so it doesn't become excessive.

Personal Care Time. Daily personal care includes such tasks as cleaning, grooming, transportation, and resting (Larson & Kleiber, 1993). Teenage girls may spend hours each day grooming. Since a child's appearance can greatly affect self-confidence and social interaction, this time is often well spent if it is not excessive; parents should help teach their children what is appropriate.

Talking. Talking represents a major activity for young adolescents. In the home environment, this often translates into time on the telephone. The amount of time girls spend talking doubles between the 5th and 9th grades. (Boys also show an increase, although it is smaller.) By the 9th grade, girls spend an average of 16 hours a week, and boys about 8 hours a week, "just talking." These figures do not include any talking that accompanies other activities such as eating, playing sports, or watching television (Larson & Kleiber, 1993). Parents must acknowledge and support this socializing activity while at the same time ensuring that it doesn't interfere with other higher-priority activities in the home.

Listening to Music. Music is popular with many youths because it is in harmony with the budding adolescent concerns of independence, romance, and sexuality—not to mention the fact that it expresses an alternative to adult concerns. Indeed, from an adolescent's point of view, as well as that of many adults, music is an antidote to and escape from the unrelenting socialization pressures exerted by family and school.

Adolescent boys tend to listen to more percussive and hard-driving rock music than do girls their age, and it appears that this music creates or facilitates more positive affective states for them (Larson & Kleiber, 1993). Generally, listening to music offers adolescents an important respite from the daily stresses of growing up.

Television Viewing Time. By the time they finish high school, most children have spent approximately 11,000 hours in school classrooms and roughly 65,000 hours outside class. Watching television easily ranks as the primary out-of-school activity, taking up roughly 15,000 hours (Medrich et al., 1982). Oddly enough, research shows that adolescents report feeling less happy, less alert, and more bored while watching TV than at other times (Larson & Kleiber, 1993). For many, television viewing seems to have become simply a bad habit.

As television viewing takes up more and more of children's free time, social scientists have become concerned with the problem of "displacement." Simply put, television viewing takes up, or displaces, time that could be spent in other activities. Bronfenbrenner argues:

> The primary danger of the TV screen lies not so much in the behavior it produces as in the behavior it prevents—the talk, the games, the family activities and the arguments through which much of the child's learning takes place and his or her character is formed (cited in Medrich et al., 1982).

Most child experts would agree that children watch too much television given the time-use options: doing other things might teach them more about their world and foster development of talents, intellect, and physical abilities. Some have even claimed that interest in television diminishes interest in other activities, actually reducing the motivation to do other things, let alone excel at them (Medrich et al., 1982).

However, in a longitudinal study, Roe (cited in Larson & Kleiber, 1993) effectively demonstrated that a person's characteristics are more likely to be a cause than a result of heavy media use. He found, for example, that heavy music listening usually does not precede a teen's poor performance in school; rather, teens who do less well in school often turn to music, perhaps as a means of reinforcing an identity that diverges from normative values. Clearly, correlational data cannot be used to jump to the conclusion that TV, or listening to music, is harmful because it precludes other activities.

A corollary research finding is that there is considerable social class variation in the amount of television viewed and in the home television environment. "Total-television households" (homes in which the TV set is on all afternoon, at dinnertime, and all evening, regardless of whether anyone is watching it) are not uncommon, particularly in less-affluent neighborhoods. Medrich et al. (1982) found that 35% of all households (21% of white, 43% of African-American) are total-television homes. It is quite possible that in the midst of negative socioeconomic conditions, some children (and adults, also, for that matter) use television as an escape from the problems of everyday life, as a source of company, and as a way of satisfying some need for fantasy. Small houses, large families, and crowded cities leave many children with few, if any, opportunities to "get away" or "blow off steam" in a socially acceptable manner. In front of the television set, a child can be "transported" beyond the problems of the immediate environment.

Adults can also be partly to blame for children's excessive TV viewing time. Consider the case of a family living in an unsafe neighborhood. For their own safety, school-aged children might be required to go home right after school and stay inside. Watching television just might be the best activity alternative in this situation, especially for children with low reading skills who find little enjoyment in books. This example illustrates the complexity of the issue. Time use by children is often the product of so many constraints that we must carefully consider our own biases and perspectives before making judgments. Unique, real-life circumstances can make choices that seemingly run counter to conventional wisdom seem very rational indeed (Medrich et al., 1982).

The bottom line on the subject is that parents need to be aware of their children's television viewing habits and must be alert for any negative consequences of excessive "tube time." Unfortunately, in only a small proportion of homes is television viewing actively monitored and other activities encouraged (Medrich et al., 1982).

A family's use of time can have important implications for the dynamics of a child's behavior. Mealtime, homework time, chore time, and other uses of time should be the subject of a clinician's assessment. Through the development of specific in-home management strategies, clinicians can attack concrete environmental factors and time-use behaviors that are frequently of primary importance in family disorganization and that are all too often ignored by treatment agencies.

Neighborhoods

The physical resources in a city naturally vary from neighborhood to neighborhood. One neighborhood might offer accessible playgrounds, libraries, etc., while another has few such resources. Another, perhaps more critical, variant among neighborhoods is the extent of informal support systems. These systems are help networks composed of friends, neighbors, and other natural helpers. Mapping neighborhood resources in relation to network supports and family needs has immense practical value in restoring the link between a family and its community. This link was carefully established and nurtured by families of earlier times, who drew more than water from the parish pump and exchanged more than produce at the local marketplace (Cochran, 1993).

Emerging evidence reveals that as neighborhoods become more fragmented and people become more isolated, people are relying less and less on friends, relatives, neighbors, and clergy for support. The deterioration of these informal support systems has recently been documented in a study in Greenville, South Carolina by Dr. Gary Melton. When residents were asked who they went to for help when they had problems, virtually no one mentioned clergy, neighbors, or relatives. In a similar study done 20 years ago, almost all respondents cited clergy or friends in the neighborhood as sources of help. In Melton's study, poorer people typically identified either "no one" or "the emergency room" as their source of help. Wealthier respondents in suburban areas often named community professionals (DeAngelis, 1993).

Families can be deeply affected by their neighborhoods and by the degree of support they receive from their neighbors and local organizations. For instance, a family that has active ties to a local church, local scouting groups, neighborhood leaders, and other neighbors tends to be more comfortable and to have a stronger sense of its acceptance in the community than a family without such connections. Children, of course, are quite aware of this acceptance, or lack of it. Families who are well-integrated into the community system are more likely to receive from it ongoing support, guidance, and confirmation of their worth (Maguire, 1991). A well-developed community "net" provides healthy social outlets for the needs and desires of family members.

For young children, the neighborhood is more than a geographical setting: it is a social universe. Since young children are only minimally mobile, the things they do from day to day are, in part, shaped by the nature of the physical environment in which they live. Streets, parks, schools, and other public amenities influence children's activity patterns in a number of ways. Likewise, the social environment of the neighborhood has a powerful impact on children's time use (Medrich et al., 1982).

Neighborhoods vary in terms of the opportunities for peer-to-peer contact they provide to children. The most systematic evidence concerning the impact of variations in the quality of neighborhood environments comes from the work of Medrich and his colleagues. These researchers isolated a number of factors, such as terrain, distance from commercial areas, child population density, and safety, that affect the number and types of social experiences that occur among neighborhood children. Based on interviews with sixth-grade children, they found that in neighborhoods in which houses are widely separated and sidewalks are scarce, children tended to have fewer friends and to travel longer distances in order to make contact with peers. Their friendship patterns were more formal and rigid. In contrast, in neighborhoods with little distance and few barriers between houses, children reported a higher number of friends and more informal and spontaneous play patterns (Medrich et al., 1982).

Safety is another neighborhood factor that can affect children's development of peer relationships. Children in neighborhoods with safety hazards, such as major thoroughfares and unregulated traffic, reported much less autonomy in visiting playmates and gaining access to play areas. Safety restraints not only limit the number of friends and the amount of large-group play, but also are associated with rigidity of friendships. Research shows that children living with such restraints often compensate by playing more with their siblings than do children in safer neighborhoods.

Finally, the density of the child population in a neighborhood is also an important factor in determining the quantity and quality of peer relationships among children. Neighborhoods with large populations of children generally provide a child with a greater number of friends, more large-group play, and more spontaneity in play. In neighborhoods with low child populations, children report having fewer friends and more formal friendship patterns (Belle, 1989).

Workplace

In the past few decades, the workplace has become one of the environments in which adolescents spend a significant portion of their time. Along with the more familiar settings in which adolescents come to maturity, workplaces now help give meaning to the lives of many adolescents and help them develop self-assurance, independence, and, ideally, maturity. Taking a job is a watershed in the life of an adolescent—the first step away from total financial dependence on the family, the beginning of independence. The influence of the workplace has implications for family life, school, and peer groups (Greenberger & Steinberg, 1986).

During the 1970s, many public policy leaders across the United States became concerned about signs of increasing social deviance and lack of motivation among the nation's youth. To address the problem, a number of official panels were convened, and the President's Scientific Advisory Committee also became involved. All researchers who investigated the problem felt that part-time jobs for teenagers should be given a high priority as an inducement to 1) stay in school, 2) think about a college education, and 3) aspire to a career later on. According to a 1987 survey performed for the Monitor the Future Program, undertaken by the Institute for Social Research at the University of Michigan, 75% of high school seniors held part-time jobs, worked an average of 16 to 20 hours a week, and often earned more than $200 a month (Bachman, 1987). But is this always good for the adolescents involved? Although some research indicates that it is, other studies suggest that it is not.

In determining whether or not a job is beneficial to an adolescent, it seems that the critical point is the nature of the job itself. Greenberger and Steinberg (1986) concluded that holding the wrong type of job can be detrimental to an adolescent. Menial jobs can devalue young people at a critical time when what they need most are affirmations of their self-worth and their ability to contribute meaningfully to society. Unfortunately, in our late 20th-century society these are the types of jobs that are most available for teenagers. Almost half of the high-school seniors surveyed in the 1986 study worked as store clerks or in food service—jobs requiring few skills and almost no mental effort. In contrast, at an earlier period in our society, adolescents often apprenticed in skilled trades, helped on farms, or performed other challenging work. These types of jobs helped many teenagers make the transition to adulthood. Greenberger and Steinberg concluded that the types of jobs held by most teenagers today (1) make an adolescent's school attendance more difficult, (2) substitute a false feeling of maturity for the real thing, (3) encourage deviant behavior, including experimentation with alcohol and drugs, and (4) bring work itself into disrespect for the students.

Another harmful factor is that teenagers who work often have no responsibilities for the money they make. Their paychecks are often just spending money. This is a disadvantage when they are allowed to spend it any way they choose, without any adult guidance regarding thrift, prudence, long-term goals, and the value of a budget. Consequently, their early "affluence" fails to prepare them for the reality of later life, when an easy-come-easy-go attitude about money invites disaster.

Another negative aspect of many of today's jobs for youths is the substantial time involvement they require. Long hours spent in the workplace rob teenagers of time they could spend in better, more developmentally productive activities.

Of course, there are always exceptions. Some adolescents work at satisfying jobs in supportive environments that have a positive influence on them. Some do not spend what they make unwisely, but instead contribute to the family income or save for some long-term goal, such as summer camp or college. The difficulty is in identifying which jobs are beneficial and which are harmful and in guiding adolescents to the former. Teenagers are too often left to their own devices in deciding whether or not to take a job, without sufficient information to make informed decisions.

How can teenagers considering employment options, many for the first time, properly evaluate the way jobs, hours, wages, and tasks will affect them immediately and in the future? They must be able to rely on advice from parents, teachers, friends, and anyone else capable of guiding them. Without this guidance toward meaningful jobs, the chances are that after-school employment will do more harm than good in the long run.

What should one look for when evaluating jobs or any other experiences for adolescents? The National Commission on Resources for Youth (cited in Asp & Garbarino, 1983, p. 281), which operates a clearinghouse of successful youth volunteer programs, suggests that the following criteria exemplify good youth jobs and programs:

- They fill genuine needs for adolescents and society.
- They offer active learning in an age of spectatorship.
- They offer challenge—providing youth a chance to do something that is difficult as well as meaningful.
- They promote maturity and responsibility.
- They give adolescents a taste of the options available in the real world.
- They involve working partnerships between youths and adults.
- They offer a community experience—a sense of belonging to an extended family, and the exhilaration that comes from being associated with others in significant activities.

Parent Workplace

Any parent who has ever had an aggravating day at work will agree that it can be difficult to avoid taking a bad mood home and infecting the family atmosphere. Likewise, when one's work provides satisfying, even exhilarating experiences, the good mood usually finds its way home at the end of the work day and can influence family relations in a positive way (Parke & Kellam, 1994). The links between family life and the parents' world of work have long been of interest to researchers.

Family researchers consider child-rearing involvement by both parents to be critical in healthy child development. Greater participation by fathers is consistently related to better child development outcomes in areas ranging from academic achievement to personal identity (Cochran, Larner, Riley, Gunnarsson, & Henderson, 1990). And evidence from two studies suggests that the more hours per week mothers are employed outside the home, the smaller their children's social networks tend to be (Belle, 1989). Unfortunately, the typical workplace presents numerous obstacles to a parent's involvement in child-rearing. Excessive time commitment is only the most obvious problem—others abound. Increased participation in child-rearing depends upon protection against forced overtime, the right to care for one's sick child or take parental leave without workplace punishment, the choice of part-time work or job sharing, flexible work schedules, and other alternatives (Cochran et al., 1990).

Churches and Other Religious Institutions

Theorists and researchers have articulated a number of important benefits fostered by religion: self-esteem, control, meaning, growth, hope, intimacy and belonging, emotional release, personal identity, emotional restraint, and comfort (Pargament & Maton, 1991). Research indicates that belief in a religion and participation in religious ceremonies (communal services, for example) tend to divert youths away from high-risk behaviors (Carnegie Council on Adolescent Development, 1992). In a longitudinal study of problem behavior in youth, Jessor and Jessor (cited in Wright et al., 1993) described adolescent religiosity as providing "a personal control against problem behavior." They found that church attendance and the expression of positive religious attitudes and beliefs among high school students were related to a lower incidence of deviant behavior and to less problem behavior in general. The members and staff of religious centers, such as churches, mosques, and synagogues, can be effective resources for overwhelmed family systems.

Young people who view their religion as providing meaning to their lives tend to experience lower levels of depression than their peers who do not view their religion as meaningful. Also, researchers have noticed a positive correlation between frequent church attendance by adolescents and lower Beck Depression Inventory scores. The evidence suggests that frequent church attendance and perceptions of religion as meaningful can be positive forces in the lives of adolescents (Wright et al., 1993). Involvement in religious activities is also associated with psychological well-being. These activities can take several different forms: attendance at religious services, prayer, efforts to avoid a negative event through rituals and other activities such as reading the Bible or a focus on the afterlife, attempts to live a less sinful, more loving life, and support from the clergy and other church members (Pargament & Maton, 1991).

Religious personnel and institutions, by their very nature, seem to foster support and trust among individuals, families, and neighbors (Caplan, 1974). With this basis of trust, religion can help individuals cope with many of the hardships of life, particularly the loss of loved ones. In this way, religion can help prevent the adoption of artificial supports, such as those involving substance abuse (Pargament & Maton, 1991).

The belief in a just, loving, supportive God appears to be predictive of more positive responses to negative events (Pargament & Maton, 1991). Whether one chooses to view hope psychologically or spiritually is irrelevant; either way, it is necessary for the successful process of change. Spiritually, it can be seen as a belief in the presence of a power greater than oneself—a power that cares for and helps those in need. Hope is also a significant factor in providing motivation, which is a precursor to most successful psychological change processes (Maguire, 1991).

The findings suggest that professionals interested in implementing adolescent programs might benefit by involving local religious and spiritual leaders (Wright et al., 1993). Of course, not all denominations and churches will offer the same degree of assistance—and some affiliations, such as with cults, can be potentially very destructive. Nevertheless, adolescent involvement with the activities of parishes, churches, and synagogues can create almost instantaneous, yet strong, positive supports. Youth groups, choirs, and the innumerable small committees that develop primarily to help the religious organizations also serve to help their members. Often, there is a bonus effect: not only do the activities help the individual who participates, but also, his or her family benefits by being accepted into a larger social system. In addition to providing positive self-image and status, this acceptance frequently brings with it nurturance, affection, altruistic outlets, and other benefits (Maguire, 1991).

Schools

Students are unmistakably affected by the straight rows of desks, stratified groups, and overflowing classrooms that make up many schools today. The ecology of the school is at least as interconnected as the ecology of the planet. With this fact and the ultimate goal of educating children in mind, the school environment becomes just one more variable that can be manipulated to achieve the goal. Thoughts such as "Lamar might do better in a highly structured class versus a more informal class" or "Mary would be less likely to get into trouble if a peer tutor accompanied her between classes" characterize the new environment-oriented thinking.

School are not just places where children study academics for six or more hours a day; they are social gatherings where children learn how to get along with others. As such, schools are logical settings for intensive efforts to support children in their affective lives. More and more, the "separatist" mentality that surrounded special education programs for so long is being challenged through efforts to integrate a variety of supportive services into regular educational settings.

Knitzer, Steinberg, and Fleisch (1990) speak of the urgency of refining classroom and whole-school strategies on behalf of students with emotional and behavioral disorders. Just as children with serious emotional disturbances can be kept in their natural home environments with sufficient support and appropriate environmental modifications, they can also be maintained in regular school classrooms. All it takes is the proper focus and some necessary environmental adjustments.

The main problem with "mainstreaming" isn't the children themselves. Rather, it is that the adults involved do not understand the primacy of systemic or contextual causes of—and solutions to—children's problems in schools. Most school personnel have probably been trained in an intrapsychic, individual mode of thinking about behavioral problems. This outdated and short-sighted perspective does not prepare them for a contextual understanding of students' problems. Consequently, the standard approach to dealing with student/environment mismatches has been to remove children with "special needs" from the typical classroom environment. Unfortunately, this robs them of much of the socializing experience they desperately need.

A related issue, and probably the biggest obstacle to implementing environmental interventions in schools, is the common perception among educators that their jobs are predominantly of an academic nature. An important step in implementing meaningful interventions is to define a child as experiencing *socialization problems,* rather than psychological problems, and to perceive the help that he or she needs as basically educational rather than psychiatric. Viewing the situation in these terms not only clarifies the actual problem, but also helps identify appropriate roles for schools and school personnel who have expertise in teaching social skills (O'Callaghan, 1993).

In-School Support

It must be acknowledged that a child who exhibits a problem behavior is not necessarily *unable* to behave appropriately; more often than not, such situations arise because the child is receiving inadequate environmental support. In-school support services encompass a broad range of interventions. The goal is to construct supportive programs, unique to each child, of one or more services that enable the children to remain in the least restrictive environments. The unique program of services designed for a specific child is usually specified in the student's Individualized Education Plan (IEP), which is completed for all special education students. The services selected for a student are strategically chosen to address the child's unique ecology; the school personnel strive to identify pivotal areas of support that will affect the student's broader school experience in a positive fashion.

A few years ago, the LaGrange County, Illinois, school system initiated individualized services with interdisciplinary teams and flexible funds to provide environmental supports in schools (Katz-Leavy et al., 1992). Some of the support services used in their "WRAP Project" included:

- In-school respite for behavioral support in regular education classes.
- In-school or in-home respite with a focus on academic tutoring, homework completion, and study skills.
- In-home respite for behavioral support, supervision and assistance for parents.
- Recreation coaches to teach or support the development of sportsmanship, rules of the game, etc.
- Buddies/Big Brothers to support effective school, home, and community interactions.
- Peer support coaching and/or monitoring to foster more effective peer interactions.
- Family advocacy/family support according to the specific needs of parents and/or siblings.
- In-school tutoring.
- After-school tutoring at home.
- After-school tutoring in school.
- Facilitation of communication between the home and school.

In-school support services offer powerful intervention opportunities. A critical factor in the success of these programs is the involvement of a number of representatives from the school and the community in the development of student IEPs. This broad-based input helps ensure the identification of the most creative and appropriate support services for an individual. Furthermore, it is essential in the IEP to designate who is responsible for carrying out each type of support service and who will monitor it regularly. In-school support services can be provided alone or in conjunction with self-contained classrooms or day-treatment programs to intensify services and ensure that a student is receiving help in the least restrictive environment possible.

Pluralistic School Environments

Schools that offer diverse learning environments have taken a huge step toward meeting the range of needs of their student populations. Offering diverse classroom settings creates more niches for more pupils (Goodhart & Zautra, 1984). Prime examples of such pluralistic schools are California's Jefferson Primary School of Pasadena and P.S. 1 in Santa Monica, both of which use a combination of educational methods in unique learning environments. In these schools, a pupil is placed in a classroom only after his or her most appropriate learning environment is identified by gathering information from the pupil, teachers, and parents.

Another critical environmental resource in all schools is the human factor—the school staff. Principals, teachers, and in-school mental health personnel should be involved in the development and implementation of any intervention activities. However, in addition to these school personnel, who have the more formal roles of intervention, there are often many individuals who, because of their personality and personal style, can help in dealing with the varied problems of children. A secretary, a custodian, or perhaps a bus driver—anyone who has established some bond with a student—can be an important resource for intervention. Figure 6-1 presents a checklist of potential human resources in schools and the criteria that are important in the selection process.

Figure 6-1: School Resources for Environmental Intervention

RESOURCE	Potential source of support?	Obstacles?	Need to monitor?	PLAN
Students				
Special education teachers				
Classroom teachers				
Aides				
Speech therapists				
Guidance counselors				
School psychologists				
Assistant principals				
Principals				
Secretaries				
School nurses				
Custodians				
Bus drivers				
Cafeteria workers				
Parent volunteers				
School social workers				
Music, art, gym teachers				
School friends				

Adapted from Kerr & Nelson, 1983.

Big Schools vs. Small Schools

Barker and Gump's classic 1964 study of school size suggests that this characteristic of a school may influence children's social relationships and, in turn, support the development of different qualities and skills. Small schools tend to offer better opportunities for students to participate directly in school activities, to develop leadership skills, and to experience a sense of belonging. Larger schools, on the other hand, may challenge students more in the area of developing one's own style of forming and maintaining relationships.

Manning theory, which is based on the distinction between undermanned settings (few people to an area) and overmanned settings (many people to an area), grew out of Barker's (1968) study of big and small schools. Barker found, not surprisingly, that people whose behavior is antisocial in some sense usually do better in undermanned settings. This seems to be due in part to the fact that undermanned settings present only a few persons to deal with in comparison to the number of setting tasks. Through such settings, people with antisocial tendencies can usually be drawn into worthwhile school activities. Overmanned settings have the opposite effect—partly, it seems, because there are too many persons compared to the number of setting tasks.

Flexibility is the key to adapting overmanned settings to meet the needs of individuals. If too many students try out for parts in a high school play, the director might decide to select two casts and let them alternate performances (Wicker, 1973). Similarly, if too many musicians are interested in joining a chamber music group, they could all be accommodated by increasing the ensemble to orchestra size (Heller & Monahan, 1977). These are good examples of how modifications to the environment can help solve problems in overmanned settings.

Family–School Linkage

Many clinicians have noted the difficulty of engaging families in treatment settings outside the school. Basing intervention efforts in the school often increases the likelihood that the child's family will become involved in the problem-solving efforts. A number of factors—ranging from familiarity with the physical surroundings and general parent trust in school personnel to the fact that the services are free—make parents more likely to accept school-based services than a referral to a setting outside school (O'Callaghan, 1993). The nature and effectiveness of school-based intervention efforts often hinge on how involved the parents become. The level of involvement schools are willing and able to develop with families is equally important (Parke & Kellam, 1994).

Peers

It is also critical to involve a child's peers in intervention efforts, particularly in school. Besides enhancing the sense of community and social integration, peers can provide useful support in dealing with academic tasks or other school requirements, can provide pleasant socializing interactions, and can be sources of emotional support in the face of stressful experiences with teachers.

Peer tutoring, which has proven effective with academic subject matter, can also be applied to the teaching of social skills and to the modification of disruptive classroom behaviors. In one study, peer tutoring increased the number of social contacts and concurrently reduced the number of negative social interactions among both high- and low-status students (Greenwood, Carta, & Hall, 1988).

Extracurricular Activities

Participation in extracurricular activities often helps students find a link between school life and the real world. An ongoing study conducted for the National Center for Education Statistics has found that students who participate in extracurricular activities in high school tend to have a more positive self-image and a greater sense of control over life events than do nonparticipants. In general, participating students have higher educational aspirations, and they are more likely to seek help from adult family members, school personnel, and friends in planning their school programs and later careers. They are also more likely to consider getting involved in community leadership and working to correct social and economic inequalities to be important life goals (Erickson, 1988).

The Carnegie Council on Adolescent Development (1992) found a correlation between student participation in extracurricular school programs and improved math and reading scores. The "Blues in the Schools" program in Charleston, South Carolina has provided much evidence of this correlation. The idea behind the "Blues in the Schools" program is to present students with a new, exciting, and relevant activity—in this case, the study, writing, and performance of blues music—but also to require that they perform as well in their schoolwork as in the extracurricular activity. Teachers and counselors help select the students who participate in the program, usually those who are having problems in school. As long as they maintain a C average in school, these students get to jam with musician Billy Branch and his blues band after school in two-hour rehearsals that generally last much longer. Each year, the program culminates in a performance before several thousand people during the finale of the Charleston Blues Festival. Many of the 140 students who have participated to date say they have found new horizons and friendships:

> Wyatt, 15, used to be a discipline problem. Unmotivated, his grades were poor. "Now I'm not afraid to try things. My grades have improved. But I didn't realize music was so much work," he says. "It's changed my son completely around," says his mother Terry Dobbs. "He didn't really care before. Now he has more respect for his teachers; he plays the guitar and stays out of trouble" (*Raleigh News & Observer*, November 26, 1993, p. 24).

Conclusion

It is crucial for clinicians to be aware of the effects of behavior settings. For example, the finding that certain behavior setting arrangements have a great impact on friendship patterns can have important implications for the treatment of individuals (Epstein & Karweit, 1983). A clinician who is aware of this fact might ask about the housing arrangements of a client who complains of loneliness and depression, instead of diagnosing the problem based solely on the dispositional deficiencies of the client. If the client is found to be socially isolated, arrangements could be made for him or her to spend more time in behavior settings where unthreatening interactions with others occur easily.

Such environmental therapy is rarely, by itself, a solution to all problems. However, if a predisposing environmental stressor can be eliminated or circumvented, the intensity of the problem can often be diminished (Heller & Monahan, 1977).

The discussion in this chapter has focused on places—the actual physical settings in which behaviors occur. Of course, every setting becomes associated with certain activities and people that help make it unique. The next chapter explores in more detail the environmental element of activities and the ways they can serve as intervention resources.

7

Activities As Resources

Chapter Preview
- Describes how the activities that children engage in can promote prosocial behaviors and reduce high-risk behaviors
- Describes youth participation in out-of-school activities
- Describes parental involvement in children's activities
- Identifies barriers to using available activities
- Describes how professionals can arrange children's activities
- Gives an example of how engineering an activity setting can change behavior
- Identifies different kinds of community activities and their characteristics

From grades 1 through 12, approximately 40% of a child's time is discretionary—that is, not spent in school or involved with essential activities such as eating and sleeping. In today's society, this discretionary time is increasingly unstructured and unsupervised, particularly for older children. We must all be aware that the manner in which free time is spent has either a positive, a negative, or a neutral effect on a child's personal development and well-being (Larson & Kleiber, 1993). For adolescents, many risks are associated with unsupervised time, and many positive effects can be gained from participation in constructive activities. Larson and Kleiber (1993) found that while some unstructured time is essential to adolescents' healthy development, many young teens need more structure and support than they are now receiving.

Most developmental psychologists agree that children and adolescents share a common core of developmental needs. Children must have access to experiences outside the school setting that enable them to meet developmental needs through relevant activities. For healthy personal and social development, they need to test themselves, pursue new interests and develop new capabilities, sharpen skills, and have fun. Jonathan Kozol (1974) recalls his own experience:

> I remember those times. ... All of the hours that mattered most to us, in terms of passion, high stakes, daydreams and ideals ... all of those hours were "sneaked in," "unlicensed." ... We got no credit hours for them (p. xii).

The substance of a child's out-of-school life is comprised of many opportunities and constraints linked to family, peer groups, neighborhood, and broader community environments (Medrich et al., 1982). Bogenschneider and his colleagues (1990) found that in every system—whether it be family, peer group, school, work, or community—increases in protective factors or assets correlate directly with decreases in at-risk indicators. In a study with a similar focus, Benson (1991) also concluded that the more assets a child has, the lower the likelihood of high-risk behaviors. Working with the four key assets of positive school climate, family support, involvement in structured youth activities, and involvement in church or synagogue, Benson found that at-risk indicators are reduced almost on a one-to-one basis as key assets are added. These findings support the proposition that the socialization of competence takes place in the context of participation in activity settings. They also suggest that certain kinds of relationships develop within these settings through which children learn skills and attitudes.

Putting together a ribbon-winning 4-H project, working on the school yearbook, and playing guitar in a neighborhood band can all be significant activities in a child's life. Families that become involved in neighborhood Little League baseball or basketball, Girl Scouts or Boy Scouts, soccer, swimming, football, dance recitals, and other such activities within the community are providing healthy physical outlets and social connections for their children. Although it is not clear whether the correlation between such activities and better mental health is causal or not, children who are actively involved in such activities tend to be less depressed and to have better self-esteem than their peers who are not involved (Maguire, 1991).

Out-of-school activities can provide adolescents with valuable opportunities to develop self-direction, self-expression, and self-motivation. The term "transitional activities" refers to activities (such as those already mentioned) that not only are enjoyable and self-motivating for adolescents, but that also provide challenges that foster development into adulthood. Participation in sports and involvement in art or hobby organizations stand out as some of the more beneficial activities a youngster can undertake. According to Larson and Kleiber (1993), such activities perpetuate desirable aspects of childhood play in being pleasurable, expressive, and intrinsically motivating, but they anticipate the meaning systems, reward structures, and intentional, directed effort associated with mature ego functioning.

Clearly, then, appropriate leisure activities are important to the development and adjustment of healthy teenagers. Unfortunately, clinicians have traditionally all but ignored this aspect of the adolescent ecology. As with environmental therapy in general, recreational therapy, which deals with this part of adolescents' lives, is too often underrated as a legitimate and effective intervention tool.

Common Activities Among American Children

The contexts for learning outlined below encompass many typical activities in the lives of today's American youngsters, regardless of their gender, race, or social class (adapted from Carnegie Council on Adolescent Development, 1992).

- *Professionally Guided, Formal Learning Activities.* Classroom lessons and in-class tutorials are the most common forms of these activities, which are geared toward personal and intellectual growth.
- *Deliberate Out-Of-School Learning and Work Activities.* This category covers activities that provide opportunities for cognitive work away from the school setting. Homework, independent study, after-school lessons, independent tutoring sessions, part-time work, musical instrument lessons, and foreign language lessons are some of the more common examples.
- *High-Yield Leisure Activities.* This category describes activities that provide youngsters practice in reading, writing, discussing, problem-solving, decision-making, and so on. These are "leisure" activities only in the sense that they are done for fun—their effect on the real "business" of growth and development can be dramatic. Reading a book for pleasure is one example. Other examples include talking with parents about political elections, or about why it is important to get a good education, or about ways of successfully handling a problematic job situation.
- *Recreational Activities.* This category includes such diverse activities as watching television, playing games, listening to music, participating in hobbies, observing or participating in group sports, hanging out, partying, and going on family vacations.
- *Health Maintenance Activities.* Dealing with emotional, mental, and physical health, this category includes such diverse activities as going to church, praying or meditating, eating, daydreaming, sleeping, washing and grooming, and doing physical conditioning exercises.

Current Participation Levels

According to the National Education Longitudinal Study of 1988, 71% of 25,000 eighth graders sampled were involved in some type of organized activity outside of school (National Center for Education Statistics, 1990). Of those who participated, 37% were involved in non-school team sports,

34% in religious youth groups, 19% in summer programs, and 15% in hobby clubs.

Tempering these figures are more recent data indicating that although many teenagers are involved in at least one non-school organization or out-of-school activity, the average amount of time a youngster devotes to these activities is relatively small (Larson & Kleiber, 1993). Other research indicates that most adolescents are not involved in any community activities on a regular basis (Heath & McLaughlin, 1991).

Common Activities Among Successful Students

Studies involving talented students have shed some light on the productive use of out-of-school time. These youngsters spend approximately 20 to 35 hours a week in various high-yield leisure and deliberate learning activities. Instead of just socializing or hanging out, they and their friends tend to choose more active and challenging pursuits, such as hobbies and group studying.

Turning learning into a "flow" experience appears to be especially important to high-achieving students. "Flow" is a subjective state that people experience when they become completely involved in an activity to the point of losing track of time and losing awareness of everything except the activity itself. People find this depth of involvement enjoyable and intrinsically rewarding. Many athletes reach the flow state during their competitions, and it elevates them to a higher level of perception and performance. It is something anyone can attain, however, perhaps when reading a well-crafted novel, or playing a good game of squash, or taking part in a stimulating conversation. A state of flow can be achieved during almost any activity, be it play, work, study, or religious ritual, as long as the conditions are conducive to it (Csikszentmihalyi, Rathunde, & Whalen, 1993).

For young children, it is widely accepted that their play is their "work." Through their play they encounter the stimulation necessary for healthy growth and development. Perhaps considering an older child's out-of-school time as "free time" is unwise, for adolescents also must receive appropriate stimulation for their healthy growth and development. Parents must realize that all children, teenagers included, often need guidance and encouragement in choosing worthwhile "free-time" activities. Support from parents can be a critical factor in ensuring that youngsters experience a variety of settings that provide adequate opportunities for social interaction.

Little data exists on how adolescents in different clinical categories use their free time and on how the activities they choose are interrelated with their psychopathology. The scant research that has been done on this topic indicates that individuals with emotional disturbance are less involved in the more favorable types of free-time experiences (sports, social interaction, and organizations) and tend to spend more time in solitary activities, such as watching television. Using their free time for such meaningless activities hurts these at-risk youths in two ways: it hinders their struggle to get through each day, and it deprives them of a wide variety of experience that is important to their psychological development. For some, drug use and delinquency might represent antisocial efforts to fill time and experience the enjoyment that others find in more prosocial activities (Larson & Kleiber, 1993).

Unfortunately, in today's society, many adolescents' free-time schedules are filled with developmentally "empty" activities. Clark (1988) compares this activity imbalance to an imbalanced diet, and the results can be analogous also. "Twinkies-chips-and-candy"-type activities do not promote healthy psychosocial development.

Parents' Involvement in Arranging Activities

The way a child uses out-of-school time is an important factor in shaping the child's attitudes and behaviors, and parents must accept their role in guiding their children toward activities with positive effects. Young children, in particular, depend almost solely on their parents to provide opportunities for social contacts. Many factors are involved, including the choice of neighborhood, the availability of child-centered activities (clubs, scout groups, sports, etc.), the accessibility of day-care or preschool facilities, and the presence of other children for frequent informal contacts.

Although some parents get an opportunity to participate in their children's out-of-school activities as coaches, den parents, and other such facilitators, most parents are relegated to the positions of "signing agent" (registering the child for teams and lessons), "taxi driver," and "cheerleader." Research has shown that parent involvement and support, even at the most basic level, are important factors in a child's length of involvement and success in an activity or organization. Furthermore, it is far more helpful to a child for his or her parents to become involved in activities themselves, rather than just telling the child what to do (Erickson, 1988).

Family helping projects, in which parents and children work side by side giving help to people in need, represent another type of out-of-school activity that promotes positive development. Habitat for Humanity projects—particularly appropriate for teenagers—are expanding into many communities across the nation. Appropriate for children of all ages are such simple activities as helping elderly neighbors with their weekly shopping or visiting someone isolated in a rest home. Students who participate in these types of helping behaviors on a weekly basis are less likely than non-helpers to exhibit risky behavior (Benson, 1991).

There are marked social class differences both in children's utilization of community organizations and in the level of maternal participation. By virtue of their purchasing power and their ability to manipulate the system, middle-class mothers are better prepared to act as social agents, and to introduce their children into the broader range of organized activities and resources beyond the boundaries of their homes and schools. Children in working-class families are only half as likely as their middle-class peers to participate in activities at all, and are less likely to participate on a regular basis. Middle-class mothers are also more likely than working-class mothers to sign their children up for formal programs.

There are also noticeable gender differences in the extent to which parents become involved in certain settings. For example, mothers communicate more regularly with child-care staff than fathers, and have more regular contact with their children's teachers in elementary school. Likewise, mothers tend to be more involved in coordinating and communicating with other social institutions. Through activities in the PTA,

Brownies, Cub Scouts, and the like, a mother helps both to maintain the communal social network and to integrate her child or children into it. Hence, middle-class American mothers today perform a disproportionate share of the mediation between the community and the family; for the most part, they are the ones who help their families adapt to the external system. Through such efforts, children receive access to a wider ranger of social activities that may, in turn, contribute to their social and cognitive development.

Generally, as a child gets older, the parents tend to play a decreasing role as active arrangers of the child's social contacts. Whereas direct observation and tracking of a child's activities are often the norm in the preschool period, mere awareness of a child's social plans and activities is more common during adolescence.

Barriers to Arranging Available Activities

Although most parents feel that the way their children occupy their out-of-school time is important, it is difficult for many parents to translate this belief into strategies that affect what their children actually do. Parents are not solely to blame for this. According to Medrich et al. (1982), "Time use itself is not the singular responsibility of anyone—it is the product of relationships among parents, children, child-serving institutions, and the broader society" (p. 54). Lipsitz (1986) has identified some of the primary obstacles to having youngsters participate in out-of-school community activities, as detailed below.

Lack of safety. The concern cited most often by parents who keep their children out of community activities during after-school hours is a lack of safety. In some neighborhoods, it is not safe for children to walk to and from after-school programs, even those that are just several blocks from the school or home. Parents who are faced with this type of environment are likely to instruct their children to go straight home after school, lock the door, and turn on the television set to alert potential intruders that someone is at home.

Lack of transportation. Lack of transportation can limit children's access to out-of-school activities, particularly in rural and suburban areas. Youngsters simply cannot get to the programs when they begin (or, just as limiting, cannot get home from them when they end) if there are no parents or other adults available at the right time to provide transportation. This is one of the few situations in which some poorer, urban children may be more advantaged than wealthier, suburban children, because public transportation can give them access to activities that attract them.

Lack of transportation is one of the most serious barriers to children's participation in after-school programs. Programs that can afford a van or a bus can alleviate many of the safety concerns and transportation problems faced by parents, but few programs have adequate funds to do this.

Lack of financial resources. Another factor that can limit access to programs and activities is the lack of financial resources. In one study, Medrich et al. (1982) found that 28% of sixth-graders were involved only in organized activities that were free of charge, and 19% were involved only in activities that charged fees. These two groups were clearly defined by family income. Given this disparity, a real problem occurs in communities that provide no free activities for youths. Of parents who leave their children alone at some time during out-of-school hours, 47% said they do so because they cannot afford to do otherwise. While the issue of children being on their own crosses income boundaries, the cost of supervision and enrichment takes its heaviest toll on low-income families, who may be unable to pay the fees associated with many after-school programs and activities.

Lack of information. A final access issue is a lack of information about existing after-school programs. Some cities and counties have resource and referral networks for parents seeking child care for young children, but no such networks are available for parents of older children. According to the Center for Early Adolescence's parent survey, parents' primary source of information about after-school activities are the messages their children bring home from school. These messages often are unreliable and rarely inform parents about the range of options available in the community. Often, the extent to which a parent can locate or encourage participation in organized activities is a function of the amount of information received (Medrich et al., 1982).

While it may seem obvious, it bears saying that one serious obstacle to using available services is a lack of available services. This is the ultimate limiting factor for parents and children seeking activities and programs to fill out-of-school hours. Many parents find few or no programs geared to the needs and interests of their children. In some rural areas, activities are simply not available, regardless of cost.

Professionals' Involvement in Arranging Activities

Professionals seeking to introduce activity-oriented interventions for a youth should first conduct a needs assessment. It is important to identify interventions that will significantly affect the child's time use outside school in positive ways. Various types of interventions that might be appropriate include (1) changing the pattern of use of existing activities, (2) identifying new activities, (3) strengthening existing activities, (4) expanding involvement to new areas within existing activities, and (5) developing well-planned mechanisms to make activities more accessible to the child and the child's family (Maguire, 1991).

Having a child join an already existing group (such as a sports team, club, or hobby group) can offer many advantages. Not only do such groups encourage social interaction through the sharing of common interests, but they also constitute ready-made social support systems. Professionals who help develop an out-of-school activity plan for a child must be sure to address the child's specific needs. A successful plan will build slowly on successive positive attachments, and it should eventually provide connections to a wide variety of activities (Maguire, 1991).

Of course, youths have their own ideas about what kinds of activities are best. According to the Carnegie Council on Adolescent Development (1992), youths routinely mention the following as elements of good community programs:

- Young teens consistently list "fun" and "friends" as the two major factors affecting their decisions about whether or not to participate in community programs. They want to be involved in activities that they perceive as being fun, and they don't want to be involved in groups in which they don't know anybody.
- Other issues of interest to both youths and their parents in evaluating a potential program include: Does the program offer interesting activities? Is the program in the proximity of the youth's home or school? If it is not nearby, is transportation offered? Is the program affordable?
- Safety is often a major concern, particularly in urban areas: Can youths get to and from the program safely? Are they assured of safe conditions at the program itself?
- Subtler issues of program philosophy and environment also come into play in the selection process: Does the program offer some measure of autonomy? Are the young people treated with respect? Are the staff members friendly, and do they care about kids? (Carnegie Council on Adolescent Development, 1992, p. 77)

According to Larson and Kleiber (1993), enjoyment and challenge provide the first criterion for evaluating a free-time experience: "A child who has at least one activity that is absorbing enough to engage his or her interest will find it easier to get through the day" (p. 22).

Engineering an Activity Setting to Change a Specific Behavior

Imagine that you are a quiet and overly disciplined administrator who would like to become more sociable and easygoing. One way to achieve this transformation would be to take up an activity that will help you change from the way you are to the way you want to be. A businessman with a Type-A personality might take yoga classes to reduce tensions.

The activity you choose does not necessarily have to appeal to you in order to work (Gavin, 1989). Take 12-year-old Rodney, for example. When his parents were divorced recently, he became depressed and also became a behavior problem at school. When school officials reacted by placing him in a special education classroom "for retards" (Rodney's words), Rodney's self-esteem plummeted. His school counselor, who saw him giving up and becoming passive, arranged for him to attend an activity after school twice a week, and not just any activity—bodybuilding. Rodney initially balked at the bodybuilding class, claiming he felt like a klutz. To provide support and encouragement, the counselor arranged for a classmate of Rodney's to participate with him. After a few weeks, Rodney began to shape up, and he developed a crush on the adult female instructor. His confidence grew, and classmates began to treat him differently after he impressed everyone with his weightlifting ability in gym class.

Gavin cautions that in choosing a "mismatched" activity to help facilitate change, it is important to build in enough support for the child to stay on track until the change becomes self-rewarding. In the case study presented, weightlifting was not a sport Rodney was interested in. The school counselor provided the critical support, working hard to ensure that Rodney attended the class. Once Rodney experienced success and new self-respect, self-motivation took over. Rodney's weightlifting offered an additional benefit not found in most activities in that it also helped to reduce tensions.

Gavin also cautions against jumping from one extreme to another. For example, in Rodney's case, a highly competitive activity would probably have been too drastic a change. A succession of gradual changes is more likely to help a child make the transition from a present situation to one that is psychologically healthier.

Finally, Gavin reminds us that introducing a new activity is not the only intervention option and may not be the best. In Rodney's case, for example, the counselor might have worked with the gym teacher to get Rodney more engaged in gym class, in which he rarely participated actively. If Rodney had been allowed to attend gym class early to help the teacher set up the equipment and prepare the activities, this leadership role might have enhanced his status among his classmates, increased his self-esteem, and diminished his depression. This intervention option of expanding one's involvement to new areas within existing activities is often highly effective.

In addition to changing behavior, an activity also may replace one. For example, activities such as mountain biking and in-line skating can fulfill an important need for some people—the need for variety, challenge, thrills, and self-testing. Recent research on the "Type T" personality by psychologist Frank Farley suggests that if individuals with high levels of such needs cannot meet them in appropriate and socially acceptable ways, they may seek thrills through dangerous and socially costly pursuits such as drug-taking, reckless driving, gambling, and criminal behavior (Roth & Constantine, 1995).

Community Involvement in Arranging Activities

Wynn and her colleagues (cited in the 1992 report of the Carnegie Council on Adolescent Development) defined community supports as follows:

> Community supports are both informal and the organized resources within communities that contribute to the physical, emotional, cognitive, and social development of individuals. Community supports include (1) opportunities to participate in organized, ongoing groups, (2) avenues for contributing to the well-being of others, (3) sources of personal support, and (4) access to and use of community facilities and events including museums, libraries, parks, civic events, and celebrations (p. 36).

The Carnegie Council on Adolescent Development (1992) notes that community supports for children were once more plentiful and effective than they are now. Over the years, the developmental infrastructure of communities has been eroded. A community's developmental infrastructure consists of

> community activities and events [children] participated in several decades ago, of adult mentors and role models who influenced the course of their lives, of central places in their neighborhoods where young people could congregate and

socialize (Carnegie Council on Adolescent Development, 1992, p. 37).

In a study of adolescents in ten American communities, Ianni (1989) found that adolescents tended to be more successful in communities whose major institutions offered consistent support during the teen years.

Because lack of parental support is one of the six characteristics associated with high-risk behavior in adolescents, many youth development programs conceptualize their role as *in loco parentis*. This rarely means that they seek no relationships with parents and other family members; rather, it tends to mean that the primary focus of their attention is on the broader needs of the young people themselves. Family involvement occurs on occasion, on an as-needed and often individualized basis. Programs that adopt an *in loco parentis* role often provide intensive services for youths—perhaps as many as 30 to 40 hours of programming per week, including meals and transportation. Such programs may also provide guidance and support during personal and family crises (Carnegie Council on Adolescent Development, 1992).

Communities today should look to their past and be more responsive to the developmental needs of youths. Clinicians should realize that it is in their best interest to help establish and mobilize better community activities. Infusing communities with a sense of responsibility for their members is the baseline starting point. Only after this sense of community is established can the focus shift to providing the resources needed to fulfill community responsibilities to youths (Combrinck-Graham, 1990).

Social and Community Service Activities

Research has demonstrated gender differences in attitudes toward and actual performance of social and community service. Unlike boys, girls tend to have attitudes that reflect high levels of altruistic, prosocial values; they are also more inclined than boys to devote time to social and community service. Community service projects planned and organized by young people themselves can provide excellent settings in which to overcome these gender barriers. Unfortunately, even youngsters who are inclined to help often lack opportunities for community service. With some adult impetus and guidance, many community needs/problems could be tackled by a teenage task force. Building neighborhood parks for younger children, planting trees or reclaiming trash-ridden streams, and registering adults to vote are examples of real projects that have engaged the skills and attention of early adolescents in various communities across the country. More communities need to tap the valuable resource of youngsters with budding social consciousness.

Both short-term and long-term studies have confirmed that adolescents engage in and learn from such civic-oriented opportunities. In a study in which ninth-grade students were randomly assigned either to a 10-week community service project or to a control group, project participants showed a reduction in alienation, isolation, and rates of discipline referrals (relative to their initial ratings) both during and after the project. Their peers in the control group exhibited no significant change. In another study that assessed 27 experiential learning (hands-on-activity-oriented) programs in secondary schools, the researchers found significant changes, relative to controls, in measures of the participants' self-esteem, moral reasoning, social and personal responsibility, empathy, and attitudes toward adults and the community (Larson & Kleiber, 1993).

In various forums across the country, America's youth have voiced the need for more regular contact with adults who care about and respect them. Programs such as The Learning Web in Ithaca, New York, are beginning to respond to this call. This program matches young people who wish to learn particular skills with adults willing and able to teach them (Ianni, 1989). The challenge is to link such initiatives with young people's desires for protection from the hazards that surround them (drugs, gangs, violence, etc.), for greater access to constructive alternatives to these hazards, and for more opportunities to make positive contributions to their communities. Young people say that they want to participate in community programs and to play active roles in selecting and designing these initiatives. They want to be viewed as partners with adults, sharing both leadership and responsibility (Carnegie Council on Adolescent Development, 1992).

Youth Development Organizations

Youth development organization is a catch-all term that is often used to refer to any group that provides organized out-of-school activities. The word "organized," as used here, means that the activities offered are supervised by adults and are administered by some agency or formal organization. "Activities" encompasses clubs, groups, teams, squads, lessons, extracurricular school programs, and the like. You can imagine the diverse options available: organizations based on hobbies and special interests, organizations that focus on sports and school subjects, organizations that celebrate ethnic heritage, organizations that help prepare one for a particular career, patriotic organizations, religious organizations, political organizations, conservation groups—and the list goes on.

Categories and Objectives

The Carnegie Council on Adolescent Development (1992) recognized the following categories of community-based youth development organizations:

- Private, non-profit national organizations that serve youth (including organizations that are primarily or exclusively youth-serving in their focus as well as multi-service organizations that offer a substantial amount of programming for youth).
- Local, grass-roots youth development organizations that are not affiliated with any national structures
- Religious youth organizations.
- Adult service clubs, sports organizations, senior citizen groups, and museums that run youth programs.
- Selected public sector institutions, such as libraries or parks and recreation departments, that offer youth services (p. 44).

Despite the wide diversity of programs, many of them share common objectives and goals, some of which are summarized below (adapted from Erickson, 1988, p. 103):

Individual Objectives
- Developing the highest possible physical, intellectual, social, emotional, and/or moral development.
- Developing self-confidence through the mastery of skills and situations.
- Developing self-awareness and increased self-esteem.
- Expanding horizons through new experiences.
- Providing opportunities for career exploration and for the development of good work attitudes and habits.
- Developing a concern for the welfare of others and for the institutions of society.
- Developing leadership skills and responsibilities; teaching the planning and management of time.
- Developing an interest in the natural environment and concern for its use and preservation.

Group Objectives
- Providing opportunities for meaningful service to the community.
- Bringing youth and adults together in a setting where they may communicate with and learn from each other.
- Providing a forum for the discussion of youth concerns and problems; serving as advocates for youth on the formation of public policy.
- Strengthening family life by supporting values held to be important and providing activities that may be shared within the family.
- Providing a peer group in which friendship can develop and grow, and where there is opportunity for shared fun and cooperative work with others.
- Providing experiences in democratic decision making, the basis of citizenship.
- Providing channels of expression through which like-minded individuals may present and transmit their views.

It is important to understand that the size of a program has little or no correlation with its effectiveness. Formally structured organizations and activities such as 4-H clubs and adult-supervised team sports are often the most popular and the most visible in many communities. However, Heath and McLaughlin (1991) suggest that small informal programs, which are often low-profile, may be among the strongest and most relevant services provided in some inner-city neighborhoods.

Structure and Content

The Carnegie Council on Adolescent Development (1992) found that most community-based organizations and programs for youths share common features. It is typical for such organizations to rely on small-group structures for most of their program delivery, and to rely heavily on the efforts of committed adult leaders (both paid and unpaid), who often double as role models and mentors. For the most part, youth participation is voluntary. Most of these types of organizations use a process methodology that emphasizes cooperative learning, peer leadership, age-appropriate programming, experiential education, and values-oriented content. The Council also identified five general content areas for the majority of programs:

- *Health and physical well-being:* Health education (including substance abuse, sexuality, and AIDS education); health promotion; health services; sports; physical fitness; other recreation.
- *Personal and social competence:* Life skills training; independent living skills; individual and group counseling; peer education and counseling; mentoring; interpersonal relationship skills, including conflict resolution; child and sexual abuse prevention.
- *Cognitive or creative competence:* Academic tutoring; homework clinics; English as a second language; communications skills; computer skills; visual and performing arts; culture and heritage.
- *Vocational awareness and readiness:* Career awareness; job readiness; job skills training; internships; summer jobs; in-house paid employment.
- *Leadership and citizenship:* Community services; community action; leadership skills training; youth advisory boards (Carnegie Council on Adolescent Development, 1992, p. 79).

One study by Csikszentmihalyi and Larson (1984) helped identify what activities youth most enjoy. As mentioned in Chapter 5, the researchers asked a group of youngsters to carry electronic pagers and self-report forms with them at all times; at forty randomly chosen moments during a week, each youngster was beeped and asked to fill out a report form. The forms involved a series of questions: Where are you? What is the main thing you're doing? Who are you with? As you were beeped, did you wish you were doing something else? What skills and/or challenges were involved in the activity? What were you thinking about? How would you describe your mood? Your energy level?

Interestingly enough, the study results indicated that the students who participated were not particularly happy watching television, resting, or idly chatting. Judging from their responses, the activities they liked best included participating in sports and working on their hobbies. They felt most alive when involved in these and other highly structured activities, in which they used their skills to pursue definite goals and in which they received clear feedback on their progress.

This study corroborated other findings concerning this age group. Adolescents tend to be product-oriented—they like to create something tangible that signals accomplishment. Consequently, most activities that adolescents elect to join yield a recognizable "product." It could be a performance, a team record, a newspaper, an edited volume—anything the youth can hold up or point to as an accomplishment. These kinds of activities often involve carrying the effort through a series of discrete steps, each of which serves as a progress checkpoint. In this way, the activities provide individuals with opportunities to set goals, launch long-term projects, and monitor the cumulative success or failure of their actions. Larson and Kleiber (1993) have found that having experiences of setting goals, acting on them, and evaluating progress toward their achievement helps individuals achieve a sense of direction and control in their lives.

In reviewing the evaluation literature on youth development programs, the Carnegie Council on Adolescent Development (1992) found that such programs can promote prosocial behaviors and reduce high-risk behaviors, as noted below:

Prosocial Outcomes Promoted by Youth Development Programs
- high educational attainment
- subsequent involvement in voluntary organizations
- participation in the political process as adults
- ability to work well with others
- development of career objectives
- increased willingness to learn
- reduced need for supervision
- highly developed personal and social skills
- advanced vocational skills
- appreciation of and dedicated involvement in community service
- leadership skills
- self-confidence
- knowledge about self and the community and its resources
- positive self-image

High-Risk Behaviors Reduced by Youth Development Programs
- teen pregnancy
- failure in school
- school suspension
- dropping out of school
- problem drinking
- associating with peers who smoke or take drugs
- sexual experimentation
- unsafe sex
- poor school attendance
- low scores on job readiness tests
- low math and reading scores
- poor self-esteem
- drug trafficking

(Carnegie Council on Adolescent Development, 1992, p. 128).

Professionals use a number of factors to evaluate the appropriateness of activities for youths. Clark (1988) has developed a four-element paradigm that can be applied in the evaluation process. There is a close relationship between the first two elements: the amount of time spent on a particular learning task, and the extent to which the child has an opportunity to use reasoning and problem-solving while engaged in the task. The third element is the extent to which knowledgeable adults have a chance to interact with the youths, and the fourth element has to do with the hidden (or not so hidden) rules, standards, expectations, and goals that surround the implementation of the activity. With the help of these or similar guidelines, professionals can confidently select intervention activities that not only engage youths but that also contribute to their healthy development.

Youth Sports

The Carnegie Council on Adolescent Development (1992) identified six types of youth sports programs that are popular in the United States today: (1) agency-sponsored programs, (2) club sports, (3) recreation programs, (4) programs sponsored by national youth organizations, (5) intramural programs, and (6) interscholastic programs. A report from the United States Office of Technology Assessment (1991) enumerates the following potential benefits youths gain from participation in organized athletic programs:

- appropriate use of discretionary time
- potential for adult guidance
- possible reduction of subjective stress
- opportunities for learning life skills and social competence
- opportunities for work
- possible reduction of substance abuse

Given the many potential benefits that can be derived from participating in athletic activities, it is disturbing to note that approximately 80% of all children drop out of organized sports programs between the ages of 12 and 17 (Larson & Kleiber, 1993).

Despite the relative scarcity of scholarly writing on the subject, youth sports environments do provide a major ecological context for the development of today's youth. Although not necessarily unique in their socialization impact, youth sports experiences assume disproportionate significance in the psychological and social development of some children today. In addition to the time drain of the practices and games associated with the activities themselves, these types of activities frequently dictate the scheduling of family life, affecting everything from mealtimes to carpooling to other adult involvement. Unfortunately, the time spent in such endeavors does not necessarily correlate with the benefits gained. Although for some children youth sports experiences may indeed be extremely positive and psychologically enhancing, for others they may be negative and psychologically damaging. The parameters that determine these outcomes warrant systematic investigation (Reppucci, 1987).

The subjective feature that most sets sports apart from other leisure activities is the experience of challenge. Youths report that sports provide a level of challenge similar to that of studying or taking a test. In their 1993 study, Larson and Kleiber found that affect during sports activities was higher than during all other activities, and adolescents reported feeling more motivated to be involved in sports, compared to other activities.

Conventional wisdom holds that participation in athletics helps build character, promotes "healthy" competition, encourages teamwork, and provides youngsters with an area of instrumental achievement unavailable to the non-athletically inclined. Studies have even shown that high school students who participate in sports often display higher academic achievement and greater educational aspirations. On the downside, it also appears that those athletes who do not diversify their interests to include other activities besides sports do not fare well in the long run (Larson & Kleiber, 1993).

For an athlete with the wrong focus, athletic competition can degenerate into a no-holds-barred effort to better the opponent. To help prevent the development of such an unhealthy mindset, applied sport psychology and coaching practice are placing increasing emphasis on the value of personal goal setting, task involvement, effort, and improvement as the cornerstones of athletic competition. Establishing performance goals and striving to meet them enables youths to stay focused on the activity, rather than becoming obsessed with beating their opponents or winning the contest. Emphasizing personal development in this way has been shown to enhance motivation, performance, and the quality of the experience for young athletes (Larson & Kleiber, 1993).

Bess (1994), in her poignant book about a school for homeless children in Seattle, describes how she engineered the involvement of one of her students in a summer basketball program. In the vignette outlined below, she encounters the coach after the boy, Alex, has had a rough day:

> "Alex has gotten a little too aggressive," his coach said. I explained Alex's territory problem ... Then Alex's coach said with great compassion, "He's definitely different ... What can I do?"
>
> He really hasn't been talked to enough, I offered. "Just yelled at. If you get down at his level and explain things, he's a good listener." The coach nodded with new understanding and returned to the court. I looked over later to see him on one knee beside Alex, talking to him, listening, nodding his head. I could see Alex warming up to him. ... That night Alex told me he thought his coach was one of the coolest people he'd ever met (Bess, 1994, p. 61).

The story goes on to recount how participating in that summer basketball program taught Alex a lot about life: what some rules were for and how they can work for you; that if you work hard, you get rewarded; that honesty can bring greater rewards than deceit. According to Bess, Alex learned mostly "that there were people in this world who love kids, no matter how they look and where they live—even if they sometimes break the rules" (Bess, 1994, p. 64).

Some researchers have explored the relationship between playing sports in an organized context and playing in the less formal settings that frequently arise when two or more children get together to play on their own (Medrich et al., 1982). One study that contrasted the effects of participation in informal sports (such as "pick-up" basketball games) with the effects associated with formal, adult-organized sports found that the former tend to foster greater openness, freedom, joking, and positive feelings; the latter were associated with higher concentration and a closer identification with group goals (Larson & Kleiber, 1993).

Educational Benefits

Educators and all professionals involved in youth development must recognize the close connection between in-school performance and out-of-school activities (Clark, 1988). It is impossible to devise strong strategies to improve children's scholastic achievement without understanding the function and substance of out-of-school time use (Medrich et al., 1982). Clark's research shows that children who have a chance to participate in "high-yield" out-of-school activities generally do better in school than their peers without equivalent extracurricular experiences:

> I have discovered that we can more accurately predict a youngster's success or failure in school by finding out whether or not he or she typically spends approximately 20 to 35 hours a week (of the 60 to 70 waking hours a week that are available to a youngster) engaging in what I call constructive learning activity. In a given week, this would consist of 4 or 5 hours of discussion with knowledgeable adults or peers, 4 or 5 hours of leisure reading, 1 or 2 hours of writing of various types (whether writing grocery lists, writing in a diary, taking messages on the telephone, or writing letters), 5 or 6 hours of homework, several hours devoted to hobbies, 2 or 3 hours of chores, 4 or 5 hours of games ... that require the player to read, spell, write, compute, solve problems, make decisions, and use other cognitive skills and talents transferable to school lessons. This constructive learning activity also includes exposure to cultural activities, theater, movies, and sports (Clark, 1988, p. 4-5).

Taken together, activities such as these represent a vast, informal system of education through which children learn a broad spectrum of skills, attitudes, and values that can support and enhance in-school learning activities (Erickson, 1988). Unfortunately, the young people who would receive the most benefit from these types of activities are usually the least likely to seek them out. Consequently, teachers, counselors, and administrators must be proactive, creative, and persistent in steering youngsters toward investing their out-of-school time in extracurricular lessons, groups, clubs, and activities (Medrich et al., 1982).

Conclusion

Leisure activities fill a sizable chunk of adolescents' time: 40% of waking hours for high school students and close to 50% for younger adolescents. More importantly, these activities are regular and predictable sources of pleasure and enjoyment in adolescents' daily lives. Participating in sports, socializing with friends, or becoming involved in a club introduces youths to settings and experiences that can be high points in their lives. Such activities can be invaluable outlets and avenues for at-risk teenagers. These experiences are often what teenagers look forward to, what gets them out of bed in the morning, and what sustains them through times when school stress or family tensions fill their lives with dread. Because leisure activities play such an important role in adolescents' lives, they deserve more attention from mental health professionals, both in practice and in research.

Quite apart from mental health concerns, free-time activities often provide a forum for the development of instrumentality. Because of their relative freedom from constraint and coercion, they provide an opportunity for exercise of initiative, expression of personal interest, self-formulation of goals, and the learning that comes from long-term investment in a self-defined project. Whereas other aspects of adolescents' lives demand accommodation (from school assignments to parental rules and job requirements),

> free-time activities, as the heir of childhood play, provide opportunities for assimilation into the adolescent's own structures and the elaboration of these structures in terms of a per-

sonally meaningful construction of the world (Larson & Kleiber, 1993, p. 92).

Additional evidence is needed to broaden our understanding of what types of activities are most likely to be effective with individual children and with particular groups of children. However, the value of activities as intervention resources is indisputable. Clinicians should be ready and willing to implement this powerful option.

8 People As Resources

Chapter Preview
- Defines "social support" and "social network"
- Describes characteristics of social support
- Describes the consultant posture in social support intervention
- Reviews methods of social support assessment
- Outlines social support intervention steps
- Describes the community-family network approach to intervention
- Gives examples of parents' support network influence on their children
- Describes the influence of peer relationships
- Describes parents' role as facilitators of peer relationships
- Describes parents' role as supervisors and monitors of peer relationships

As mentioned earlier, dividing a child's environment into various factors of developmental influence is artificial and arbitrary. Places are of little consequence without the activities performed in them, and activities can have different effects in different contexts. Our discussion now shifts toward a focus on the "glue" that brings places and activities together and makes them meaningful in terms of child development. Although an individual can achieve some growth and development in isolation, the achievement of one's full potential and social health depends on positive interactions and meaningful relationships with other people.

Focusing on *people* as elements of environmental intervention simply means identifying individuals who are important in a child's life and bolstering their ability to act as supportive resources. The support they provide often comes through informal or unstructured means, such as providing advice or emotional support. The goal here is to maximize the potential of others to be of help and to ensure that they have the skills and resources they need to provide the assistance and support the child needs. In other words, it is all about strengthening the child's social support system.

Research has consistently revealed the benefits of a well-developed, reliable social support system. For children, a particularly critical component of this support system is their peer group. The peer group is a major social setting within which children seek to find an identity as they grow up and make the transition from childhood to adulthood. The quality of peer social support for a given child may well have an important effect on his or her adaptive success. The fact that many children today spend more time with agemates than with any other people increases the significance of peer relationships. Because this is such a crucial area in a child's social support system, issues related to friendships and to peer influence are discussed in a separate section later in this chapter.

Introduction to Social Support

Most communities have identifiable people or groups of people filling roles like the following:

- The elderly woman on the block to whom neighbors turn for emergency babysitting.
- The clergyman who listens to parishioners talk about their marital problems and worries about their children.
- The ToughLove group organized to provide mutual support for parents experiencing child-rearing difficulties.
- The neighbor who takes in a 14-year-old girl whose family has thrown her out of the house.
- The pharmacist to whom a teenager talks about contraception.

- The neighborhood organization that helps residents find child care.
- The ethnic organization that helps middle-aged parents with the strains caused by value conflicts with their children.
- The teacher who tutors a child for free after school.
- The union shop steward who helps a family obtain funds to buy a scout uniform for their child.

These examples and others like them comprise the system of support that individuals in a community rely on to help them get by. According to Caplan (1974), one of the early pioneers in the field, a social support system "implies an enduring pattern of continuous or intermittent ties that play a significant part in maintaining the psychological and physical integrity of the individual over time" (p. 7). Echoing the concept of a lasting, reliable web of support, Whittaker and Garbarino (1983) described a social support network as "a set of interconnected relationships among a group of people that provides enduring patterns of nurturance (in any or all forms) and provides contingent reinforcement for efforts to cope with life on a day-to-day basis" (p. 5). Hence, some of the defining characteristics of social support systems are: they involve positive relationships among defined sets of people; they are enduring, as families and good friendships are; and they provide encouragement, caring, and direction to individuals, particularly to those in need (Maguire, 1991).

Children require four major types of social support for their healthy development:

- *Companionship support:* Often, the simple opportunity to share activities with another person—to have a companion—is supportive. This type of support strengthens one's feeling of belonging.
- *Instrumental* or *tangible support:* the provision of resources or services that are necessary for solving practical problems.
- *Esteem support:* statements or actions that convince people of their own worth or value. This type of support has also been

called *emotional support,* because its aim is to make people feel better about themselves or their life situation.
- *Informational support:* advice or guidance that is helpful in coping with problems.

Community support systems can be a critical factor in mental health, as the following statement from the President's Commission on Mental Health (1978) indicates:

> To be connected to others, to belong, to receive social support when it is needed and to be able to give it in return is an important part of mental health. What is more significant is that utilization of social and community support systems can provide for constructive innovations and systematic change in the mental health system, moving toward a comprehensive human service system with a holistic orientation that would remedy some of the defects [in] our present fragmented and uncoordinated efforts (p. 144).

Typically, sources of support vary along a continuum that begins with the core family unit and extends outward to reach more distant individuals in the community. Even casual, informal relationships can influence children. Who they talk to and what they discuss may play an important part in molding their view of the world and how they fit into it (Larson & Kleiber, 1993).

Grandparents, uncles, and other family members, as well as neighbors and friends, can have significant effects on the psychological health and development of children. Extended family members are often significant resources, helping out when there is a need. Unfortunately, the extended family is often overlooked as an important resource. In cases in which a parent or parents are not able to care for their children, it is not uncommon to see the children removed from family altogether because this important resource is not adequately considered (Combrinck-Graham, 1990).

In identifying and evaluating potential resources in a child's social support system, it is important to recognize the difference between *social networks* and *social support networks*. The distinction lies, in part, in the fact that interactions with social network members can be stressful as well as supportive. Because of this, network members can influence mental health and development in ways that extend well beyond those included in the "support" concept (Cochran, Larner, Riley, Gunnarsson, & Henderson, 1990).

The occasional substitution of the terms "social network" and "social support system" for one another, though understandable, is technically inaccurate. Again, the term "social support system" connotes *positive* things: help, guidance, and caring provided by family members, friends, professionals, and others. Because a social network may have either positive or negative influences, in analytic studies the term is considered to be essentially neutral (Maguire, 1991).

Cochran and Brassard's (1979) definition of a social network as "those people outside the household who engage in activities and exchanges of an affective and/or material nature with the members of the immediate family" reflects the broadness and potential complexities of this interactive human web. The analysis of social networks is concerned with the linkages among persons in the set, and focuses on the connections between any two persons in the set and among all persons in the set. A more concrete way to conceive of a person's social network is to think of the person as the hub of an irregularly shaped wheel that has spokes emanating from it to various points along the rim of the wheel. Some of the spokes represent the linkages between the person and the other persons in the network, who are points along the rim. Other spokes connect the people along the rim of the wheel to each other, some of whom are directly connected to the person, and others who are connected to the "hub" person only through another person (Milardo, 1988).

Social support interventions may be used to enhance traditional treatment approaches. Treatment efforts can be made more permanent and enduring through the supportive assistance of kin, friends, neighbors, and other "informal helpers" who can help families sustain and consolidate the gains made in professional helping. A social support system is always a "work in progress." This is especially true of the support networks of children. Variables that can affect a child's support system include the parents' social network, the family's culture, the family's degree of mobility, the gender and age of the child, and whether or not the family is run by a single parent. In constructing an intervention, consultants must be mindful of all these factors.

Influences on Social Support

Parent Social Networks

The social networks of parents have the potential to influence their children's development both directly and indirectly (Cochran & Brassard, 1979). Direct influences involve changes in a child that result from face-to-face interaction between a member of a parent's network and the child. Indirect influences involve changes in the parents themselves—for example, in their child-rearing attitudes and behaviors—which in turn affect their children.

Indirect influences can reach children through any of three major mechanisms. The first is the general emotional and instrumental support provided to parents by members of their social network. A second avenue for influencing children is opened when members of a parent's network directly encourage or criticize specific parenting behaviors. A third method of influence is modeling: network members who are parents themselves can provide observable examples of appropriate and effective parenting behavior.

Cultural Values

A child's culture is an important factor in any study or assessment of the social support system. In many non-Western societies, children commonly receive nurturance and guidance from many adults other than their parents. For example, children of the Yoruba peoples of west central Africa typically participate daily in a denser, more extensive network of social relationships than their American counterparts (Salzinger et al., 1988). In some cultures, children frequently eat and sleep in the households of various relatives, spending about as much time with other kin as with their mothers (Cochran et al., 1990).

All too often in the United States today, families retreat from the outside world. Although legitimate concerns may cause this reaction, the effects on a child's development can be far-reaching. Children growing up in such families are deprived of much of the experience of the adult world. Consequently, these children are handicapped in their future adjustment to adult roles. Children who experience a greater diversity of role models are generally more adaptable and better able to function in today's complex society (Belle, 1989).

Residential Mobility

Viewing residential mobility as the natural enemy of social networks may not be justifiable. In comparing the social ties of children who had moved during the previous 3 years with those of children who had lived in the same neighborhood since they were 3 years old, Cochran and colleagues (1990) found statistically significant differences only in the white American sample. In that group, the children who moved had ties with fewer adults than the residentially stable children, and the "movers" were less likely to know adults in the neighborhood. However, mobile youth had just as many friends as children who had not moved.

Gender and Age

Evidence indicates that there are gender differences in the style of relationships within children's social networks. Girls' relationships tend to be more intimate, self-disclosing, and dyadic, whereas boys prefer larger, more superficial chum groups with friendships revolving around shared activities rather than verbal self-disclosure. During early childhood, boys appear to be more vulnerable than girls to many psychosocial stressors. This might, in part, help explain boys' reluctance to establish intimate, disclosing, and supportive relationships.

Adolescent girls tend to identify more informal sources of support and emotional comfort, such as friends and trusted adults, than do their male peers. Girls are simply more inclined than boys to seek instrumental help from others and to be comfortable with the support they receive. Although boys may also use network members in times of stress, it appears that these friends are sought out to provide alternative satisfactions and distractions from problems rather than direct emotional comforting and instrumental assistance.

Of course, age as well as gender is a factor in the makeup and style of social network relationships. The process of growth and development continually increases the complexity of a child's life-space. As children grow older, they expand their capabilities to do more things with more people in a widening variety of settings. Despite these changes, the differences noted between girls and boys generally persist through adolescence (Cochran et al., 1990).

Finally, there may be age-related differences in the relation of social support to socioemotional functioning. Looking for possible relationships between these two variables during middle childhood, Bryant (1985) carried out a cross-sectional comparison of 7- and 10-year-old children, assessing sources of support at home and in the neighborhood/community and administering several measures of socioemotional functioning. She found evidence of a positive relationship between the support variables and socioemotional functioning for the 10-year-olds, but not for the 7-year-olds.

Single Parenthood

Evidence shows that compared with mothers who have partners, single mothers experience a more demanding environment, and they are more vulnerable to the stresses created by those demands. Belle (1989) found that the emotional well-being of mothers depends less on network size, proximity of network members, and frequency of contact with those members than on the number of network members engaged specifically in providing child care assistance and serving as "someone to turn to." These two critical network assets are more common to mothers with partners than they are to single mothers. This concrete assistance from the social support system seems to carry over positively to the quality of the interactions between these mothers and their children (Cochran et al., 1990).

The most obvious difference between the personal networks of married and single mothers is that the single women's networks are comprised predominantly of non-kin members. In this study, non-kin represented a key source of interaction and support for white children in single-parent families (Cochran et al, 1990). Cochran et al. also found that divorced mothers who rely on relatives for child care assistance are generally less satisfied with the support they receive than divorced mothers who rely only on themselves or friends.

In their 1990 study, Cochran et al. also found evidence that community supports that provide single parents with opportunities for expanding their social relations—such as impromptu social visits by community members—are associated with improvement in their children's performance in school. The benefits of expanding and strengthening a family's web of social support clearly touch intrafamily relationships as well. Wahler (1980) observed, for instance, that on days marked by visits from supportive non-family adults, both mothers and children exhibited improved social behavior toward each other.

Divorce, which has escalated alarmingly over the last two decades, has always wreaked havoc on individuals' lives. In the aftermath of a divorce, children's social support systems can disintegrate quickly. In addition to the disrupted intrafamily relationships, children's peer relationships can be affected for up to 2 years after the divorce. Remarriage of the noncustodial parent often results in decreased contact between the children and that parent, and in such situations, contact between the child and the noncustodial grandparents can be seriously diminished or lost entirely. Strengthening existing social supports and establishing appropriate new ones are critical to helping children cope with divorce (Belle, 1989).

Disabilities

The social network of parents of children with disabilities are generally smaller and denser than those of other parents. More in-depth analyses have revealed that the parents of children with disabilities differ from other parents mostly in that they experience fewer contacts with friends and neighbors (Salzinger et al., 1988). Because of the time drain associated with caring for their children, parents in these families need to make special efforts to devote time to the establishment and nurturance of social supports.

Variety, Depth, and Duration of Relationships

The strength and effectiveness of a child's support system is dependent, in part, on the number of different roles represented by its members. The social networks of most children today include a parent or parents, siblings, peers, relatives, teachers, and community members. Exposure to the wide variety of people who fill these roles enables children to experience different kinds of support, different styles of interpersonal interaction, and different kinds of activities and skills that are necessary for developing social competence. Also, the support system gains strength and cohesion when one person fills more than one role. "Multiplexity," or the performance of more than one support function by network members, is associated with greater satisfaction of children with their networks.

A child's *breadth* of exposure to different types of people can be gauged by the number of different people in each role in the child's network. The closely related concept of network *range* refers to the extent to which a network brings influences from diverse social worlds. Network range is customarily measured by counting the number of network members from outside the child's town who interact with the child once a month or more. Having a broad network range is generally healthy in that it brings novel influences to the child (Cochran et al., 1990).

Another critical variable is the *depth* of a child's relationships with network members. Both the frequency and the extent of contact with a network member influence the depth of the relationship. These factors control whether the child is learning intensive or superficial modes of relating to people. These factors are also relevant in determining whether the child's exposure to people in various roles is adequate for learning what the people have to offer.

The *longevity,* or *duration,* of a child's relationships also influences the child's development. It is important for children to have some long-term relationships so they have the opportunity to develop skills for weathering the changes that occur in such relationships over time. It is equally important for them to experience meeting new people so they can develop skills for establishing and maintaining short-term relationships. A good, strong social support system will provide a child with plenty of opportunities to establish both types of relationships.

Consulting to Social Support Networks

Helping to create or modify support networks for individual children is not an easy task. To begin with, some believe that providing a child with this protective web is not always in the child's best interests. It is notable that families and communities have been handling the problems of their members, without any outside help, since the dawn of human society. Acknowledging this historical independence of social networks, yet fully confident in their abilities to lend assistance, consultants must design interventions aimed at strengthening and empowering families, neighborhoods, and religious institutions as first-line help providers.

The professional's role is to identify and develop the social supports necessary for providing the child with experiences that will promote the development of context-appropriate competence. This can only be done by consulting with and enlisting the help of members of the family's social network. In other words, the professional must empower the network to participate in and eventually assume responsibility for the "healing" process (Milardo, 1988).

Even when a consultant has good intentions and the proper focus, several cautions are in order. The child may resent any intervention designed and imposed by adults, feeling that it is intrusive, even demeaning, to be targeted for such help (Ianni, 1989). Early in an intervention program, the consultant must obtain "buy-in" from the child. The child's attitude should also be closely monitored throughout an intervention, or the success of the efforts could be jeopardized.

Professionals must also take care to ensure that any new support structures they create on behalf of their clients do not supplant or alienate natural sources of support. Supplanting natural supports is a real danger, particularly with intensive interventions such as family preservation efforts. Evidence suggests that in such situations, as time goes by, the support from natural, informal sources diminishes, possibly leaving the family more vulnerable than it was before (Fitzgerald & Illback, 1993). Furthermore, programs such as Big Brother and Big Sister may inadvertently undermine an adolescent's confiding relationship already established with an adult neighbor or a coach. Although introducing new supports such as these can yield pronounced benefits for the individual in the short run, equally dramatic negative outcomes are possible in the long run if these interventions alienate important members of the larger natural network in which the child is embedded (Gottlieb, 1983).

Obviously, professionals who design and implement interventions for children must step carefully and keep a long-term perspective. They must develop a deeper understanding of, and be sure to take into account, the interplay between the natural social conditions that give rise to support and any deliberately arranged support structures. Doing so will ensure that the intervention strategies they design are robust and ecologically sensitive and, therefore, effective.

Assessment of Social Support

A critical early step in all ecological interventions is the identification of the individual's existing support system. When a child is the subject of concern, the focus expands to include the entire family's support system. What follows is sort of a cookbook strategy for mapping a family's social support network.

First, have the family generate a preliminary list of persons, social organizations, and agencies that they have contact with on a regular basis or that they contact with specific concerns or problems in times of need. All members of the immediate family should be involved in this effort to identify every element of their web of support; even a resource used by only one family member is part of the family's system. Mapping a family's social network is an important first step because it makes it possible to identify which, if any, existing sources of support might supply the resources necessary for meeting the family's current needs (Dunst et al., 1988).

A simple, effective strategy for exploring the feasibility of using existing sources of support is to query the family about what has already been done to address the problem at hand, and whether family members have thought about other ways of meeting their needs. Some questions that might help uncover useful information include the following: *Who have you already talked to about this problem? What are you currently doing to handle this need? Have you thought about ... as a way of getting that resource?* For the child, a more appropriate question might be: *Is there anyone special, besides your mom and dad, that you like to visit and spend time with?* Asking questions such as these not only helps identify potential intervention resources, but also sets the stage for discussing the ways in which the family goes about mobilizing its support system (Dunst et al., 1988).

To assess each family member's unique connection with the social environment, it is necessary to gather information concerning the size and composition of each individual's network, the extent to which network members provide different types of support, and the nature of relationships within the network. This can be accomplished through face-to-face interviews with the family members or by using self-report social support scales. It is important to ascertain answers to several questions (adapted from Tracy & McDonell, 1991): What are the strengths and capabilities of each individual's social network? Do these resources seem adequate to meet the individual's needs, or are there gaps in the social support structure? Are supportive relationships easily accessible, dependable, and reciprocal? Is the individual surrounded by a negative, conflictive network that fosters dysfunctional rather than functional behavior? If so, is the individual capable of accessing and maintaining more supportive relationships?

When the size and composition of the family's primary network has been determined, ask the parent to select from the total network those individuals who, for one reason or another, are perceived as being the most important members.

To explore how social support systems function, consider the following case studies:

> Ten-year-old Tabitha lives with her mother and an aunt in an urban area. Her father died when she was 6, and she has no sisters or brothers. Many of Tabitha's kin live nearby, and she sees them at church on Sundays. Her mother operates a beauty salon in their house. Tabitha knows most of the neighbors, because they regularly visit her mother's salon. She is friends with numerous children in the neighborhood. She and her best friend, Sherri, earn money by cleaning a nearby convenience store after school three times a week. The elementary school Tabitha attends is only two blocks away. Twice a month her Brownie group meets there. While Tabitha has adequate supports, she may benefit from an expanded social support network that provided exposure to a wider range of people, thereby giving her a chance to develop the social skills needed in meeting people and developing new relationships.
>
> Latisha, who also is 10 years old, lives with her mother and an older brother, who is 14. Her mother never married, and Latisha does not know her father. Her mother has cancer and is often quite ill. A year ago, the family moved out of the city to a rural town to obtain available subsidized housing. Now all their kinfolk live an hour away in the city. Latisha spends much of her time helping her mother and doing household chores. Her mother's sister comes on weekends to help out, and a visiting nurse comes one day a week. Latisha's one good friend from school occasionally comes over on a Saturday to play. Her brother has many friends who visit him at the house. They often talk to her, and she enjoys their attention. For Latisha, social support will enable her to learn the skills involved in maintaining high levels of instrumental support among her kin.

The lives of these two children differ in many obvious ways, and their social support systems differ markedly also. They differ in the breadth of the girls' exposure to and access to different kinds of people; in the amount and nature of contact they have with their mothers, kin, and unfamiliar people; in the types of activities they participate in with children and adults; and in the obligations and privileges that accompany their various relationships. Along with these differences in network structure and relationship content, the girls experience the four primary types of social support—esteem, informational, instrumental, and companionship—in differing amounts or configurations.

It is tempting to ask whether one of these girls can be said to be receiving *more* social support or *better* social support than the other. From an ecological and developmental perspective, this is a meaningless question. It is pointless to try to assess the quality or quantity of social support experienced by children without considering the nature of the ecological contexts in which the children live, and the fit between the support and the context. The only valid criterion for judging the adequacy of the amount and type of support received is whether or not the support is helping the child develop the skills, knowledge, attitudes, and social connections he or she will need to become a competent person within the society in which he or she lives.

A social support system designed to meet all of an individual's needs is worthless unless the individual values and uses the various resources. Hence, a thorough assessment must take this perspective also. The concept of *network orientation* is a measure of an individual's willingness to use interpersonal resources. A person who believes that help from others is either unavailable or inadequate, or that people just can't be trusted, is characterized as having a *negative network orientation*. In contrast, individuals with a *positive network orientation* perceive support more positively, engage in more supportive interactions, and have greater resources. For adolescents, network orientation often varies depending on whether the potential sources of support are family members, friends, or important nonfamily adults (Trickett & Schmid, 1993).

Another key factor to assess, one that has already been mentioned briefly, is *network reserve*. As the term implies, this deals with untapped potential—that portion of the capacity for support contained in the existing network that is not currently being drawn upon. It is always advantageous to work within the existing network if possible, and few network resources are ever used to their full potential. Consultants must seek to uncover untapped support that will meet the individual's current needs.

How much social support is enough? Is there a certain optimal network size, beyond which no more benefit can be gained? Or is there a point beyond which the law of diminishing returns takes effect and an increase in resources actually decreases the overall support? There are no universal answers to these questions. Interventionists must attempt to discover the optimal level of social contact for each individual dealt with.

Social Support Intervention

Interventions in social support systems can take different forms and serve various purposes. An extremely isolated family that has few resources to draw upon in times of stress may need structural interventions to augment the number and types of existing supports. Other families may have trouble accessing the network resources they need for other reasons, or family members might be surrounded by conflictive relationships. In situations such as these, it may be necessary to introduce interventions designed to improve the quality and functioning of supportive relationships (Tracy & McDonell, 1991). In all cases, the interventionist must help establish strong, healthy connections between available community resources and the individuals in need of support.

Often conducted in conjunction with other treatment interventions, social support intervention is a process that complements treatment while establishing a buffer against sources of ongoing environmental stress. Social support system development is a generalist approach that can be used with mainstream psychotherapies, as well as with more formal network interventions such as community-family network therapy (discussed later in this chapter).

As noted previously, the sources of support and extrafamilial resources potentially available to a family include relatives, friends, neighbors, coworkers, church associates, clubs and social organizations, day-care centers, and any other individuals, groups, or social organizations with which the family has contact either directly or indirectly. An operational distinction is generally recognized between *informal* and *formal* sources of social support. Informal resources include both individuals (kin, friends, neighbors, minister, etc.) and groups (church, social clubs, etc.) that are accessible within the daily routine of life, usually in response to both normative and non-normative life events. Formal resources also include both individuals (professionals such as physicians, infant specialists, social workers, therapists, etc.) and groups/agencies (hospitals, early intervention programs, health departments, etc.)—the difference being that these sources of support exist *outside* the daily routine of life. They exist for the express purpose of providing aid and assistance to persons seeking needed resources (Dunst et al., 1988).

The distinction between formal and informal resources is not just definitional. Research consistently shows that regardless of the population being studied, the positive effects of support provided by informal sources generally exceed the positive effects of support attributed to formal sources (Bennett, Lingerfelt, & Nelson, 1990).

Self-help groups are an increasingly popular form of informal support. Whether they are focused on political and social action or consciousness raising and self-improvement (or whatever), these groups also provide social interaction and some degree of general support for families. Some self-help groups are specifically oriented to family concerns. There are literally hundreds of self-help groups that help families feel supported and needed while offering them an outlet for their own abilities and talents (Maguire, 1991). A partial listing of groups with this focus includes:

- Parents Anonymous, which helps parents who have been abusive toward their children.
- Lamplighters, which supports parents whose children have died.
- Alanon, Alateen, and Alatot, all of which help members of families in which there is alcoholism.

- Parents Without Partners, for single parents.
- Families of Adult Mentally Ill (FAMI), for both parents and siblings of individuals with an ongoing mental disorder such as schizophrenia

Bennett, Lingerfelt, and Nelson (1990) have summarized the sequence of specific steps to be taken in building social support for clients. The approach begins with some of the basic assessment strategies already discussed and progresses through steps designed to empower the family to monitor, nurture, and modify its own social support system to meet ongoing needs. The basic steps are:

1. *Help the family identify its personal network.* Generate a list of people, groups, agencies, and organizations with whom members of the family have regular contact or to whom they turn in times of need. This will help identify both formal and informal members of the family's personal social network.
2. *Determine what actions the family has already taken to receive support for the current problem.* Ask, "Have you already talked to a friend or relative about what's bothering you?" or "Have you thought about contacting someone at ... agency regarding this issue?"
3. *Match family needs, in order of priority, with potential sources of support.* Be sure to look first within the family itself for resources to meet needs, then to other members of the family's informal and formal support network. The family should eventually assume this task.
4. *Explore sources of support outside the family network.* When needed aid is not available from existing network members, suggest resources you are familiar with to broaden the family's potential pool of support. For example, a parent you know who has learned to cope well with her child's disability might be a good resource for another family needing guidance in managing their disabled child.
5. *Help minimize or eliminate obstacles that block access to neces-*

sary support. Sometimes a family might feel that recommended supports are not viable options because they seem too difficult to obtain or maintain. It is important to help a family overcome these secondary obstacles so they can obtain the resources necessary for meeting their original needs. For example, a parent who finds day care for her child may not be able to use this needed service if she has no way to get her child to the day care center. You might help the parent find someone already driving another child who could give her child a ride also.

6. *Determine the "cost" of seeking or accepting help.* Asking for and accepting help are complicated processes for most people. A family may have a need for which necessary resources are available, yet the perceived reliability or unreliability of the source of support, the impending indebtedness that the family will feel, and other factors influencing the "cost" of asking for help may all interfere with getting the need met. Always find out how the family feels about asking for and accepting help and what they perceive will be the response of those asked to give help. This information can allow you to explore with the family ways to manage obstacles that interfere with acquiring necessary resources.

7. *Move the family to act on obtaining identified resources.* Once existing (or even potential) sources of support have been identified, assist the family in devising a plan of action to obtain the resources. Take as much advantage as possible of the family's existing strengths and capabilities in the methods selected for carrying out these actions. In most cases, plans for obtaining aid or assistance should be contingent upon the family's playing an active role on their own behalf.

Bennett et al. (1990) also suggest keeping these important guidelines in mind when structuring social support interventions:

- In structuring supports and resources to meet needs, always look to the family unit first and then give preference to the family's

informal social network. Do not use or create a professional resource for support if the same assistance can be provided by a member of the family or the family's informal support system. The goal is always to achieve the needed support at the closest possible level to the family unit itself.
- Use professional services for support or resources that cannot be provided otherwise.
- Involve the family in the intervention by encouraging family members to take as much responsibility as possible in identifying and obtaining needed resources.
- Create opportunities for the family to develop additional skills and capabilities as they identify and acquire the support and resources they need.

Community-Family Network Therapy

Some situations seem to call for intensified intervention efforts. Cutler and Madore (1980) have identified particular situations for which community-family network intervention may be appropriate. In general, they recommend implementing this "double-strength" strategy any time two or more of the following conditions exist:

- A crisis state continues to expand with no indication that spontaneous resolution will occur.
- Increasing distress within the family is producing symptoms in more than one member.
- Multiple contacts with many agencies are yielding few or no results.
- Temporary or permanent removal of the symptomatic family member is deemed either impossible or more detrimental than beneficial.
- Family members and professionals view the problem as being potentially disastrous without a major overhaul.
- Lack of interagency coordination creates or worsens communication problems, thereby fueling the blaming process.

- Agencies working with the family feel discouraged or are resigned to the fact that they are dealing with a "hopeless" family (adapted from Cutler & Madore, 1980, p. 147).

The community-family network simply consists of the family network with appropriate community agency officials added in. Community-family network intervention is implemented by involving the family network in the planning-linking conference. This style of intervention enables clinicians to enlist as many members of the potential community network as possible on the client's behalf (Cutler & Madore, 1980). Bringing together all of these key players at the overall intervention planning stage can help untangle the individual's contacts with community agencies and reorganize what might have been disjointed and conflicting assistance into a well-structured, cohesive, and more effective program.

To initiate the intervention, the clinician must first identify everyone in the client's family and social network and all community agency leaders who have the potential to help resolve the problem at hand. A community-family network intervention naturally includes people from both sides—for example, the clinician and truant officer representing the community, and siblings and other relatives representing the family. It is also critical to determine whether there is someone the client would *not* want brought into the intervention. When the list is complete, the clinician must establish a day, time, and place, and invite all the individuals to an initial network session. This gathering, which should last no more than three hours, should be held in or as close as possible to the client's home or other familiar area—in other words, within the client's environment (Garrison, 1981).

To open the meeting, the group leader should remind all participants why they have been called together and what they want to achieve. It should be emphasized that rather than making a diagnosis or formal assessment, they are to focus on the nature of the client's problem, possible approaches to it, and the responsibility that each of them has to extend assistance. They will be reminded that nothing yet done has solved the client's problem, and that they are meeting to decide on a new approach, with each of them pitching in. This kick-off talk should be inspirational as well as practical, designed to galvanize the members into action by stressing their commitment to the client and the capacity of each of them to make a real difference in the client's treatment. The leader must be upbeat, blaming no one for the problems, commending everyone for their commitment, and assuring everyone that the chances for success are good (Cutler & Madore, 1980). Summarized below are the typical steps involved in planning and holding a community-family network session (adapted from Garrison, 1981):

1. Relevant members of the child's network and influential community agency leaders are contacted and convened for the network session.
2. The network session begins with the usual social graces (e.g., handshaking, coffee) and introductions.
3. The purpose of the meeting is defined in general terms (i.e., sharing information and discussing potential problem-solving strategies), and then any specific agenda items are announced (e.g., the child keeps running away and is disruptive in school).
4. The convener elicits from the network members a laundry list of complaints and problem definitions, which are subsequently narrowed down to specifics, then reversed from negative statements (e.g., daughter stays out all night) to goals or expectations of competent behavior (e.g., daughter will be in the house by her 10:00 p.m. curfew).
5. During the meeting, the convener and professional participants assess the network's potential as a support system and as a resource for the future needs of the child.
6. The convener ends the session by summarizing what has occurred, reviewing any specific decisions that have been made, and clarifying any assignments, or "homework." The group should also agree on a date for the next session.

Gatti and Colman (1976) found that there are a number of salient subsystems in an individual's overall environmental system. This fact can be useful to organizers of community-family networks. Especially when an individual's network is extensive, it may be better to meet different subgroups at different times, just to keep the logistics and discussions manageable and productive. If this strategy is used, then it becomes the leader's responsibility to pass information between the various groups so that everyone remains on equal footing. Breaking into subgroups is also a way of protecting family members who prefer not to have their private difficulties discussed at a full network meeting, and of dealing with cases in which some people, especially professionals, are not directly involved with the client at that time (Gottlieb, 1983).

An important note: Rarely do the conveners of a network session have the opportunity to assess the psychological status of everyone invited to participate. Consequently, it is possible that someone at the session will be exposed to intensely emotional situations that he or she has trouble dealing with. For this reason, it is strongly recommended that two facilitators be present, one in the leadership role and one focused on monitoring the group process.

The Influence of Peers

A child's *peer network* consists of those children who are important to the child, or with whom he or she interacts on a regular basis (Salzinger et al., 1988). All of our lives are enriched by our peers. Friends help us through the trivial, mundane, or wearying routines of daily life, either by trudging along beside us or by diverting our attention to more cheerful thoughts and more meaningful personal exchanges. Whether they are supportive or not, peers are often valued simply as companions (Milardo, 1988). In adolescence, in particular, as the challenges of life begin to expand exponentially, having a trusted crew of "mates" nearby is a critical factor for healthy development.

Berndt and Savin-Williams (1993) have found that adolescents who have close friendships and are generally accepted by their peers are typically more socially skilled and academically successful and exhibit higher self-esteem than their agemates who are loners. For the most part, adolescents who lack supportive friendships or who are rejected by many of their peers show poor psychological, social, and academic adjustment.

Many factors influence the quantity and quality of peer relationships. Most children grow up experiencing a number of environments, including their home, school, neighborhood, church, and after-school activity settings. The structure of each of these environments influences the types of peer relationships formed, the types of activities engaged in, and the depth of the interaction and intimacy that develops among peers. Some environments may provide many opportunities to interact with numerous other children; other environments may provide few or none at all. The structure of an environment may encourage or even mandate interactions, or it may prohibit or constrain them. Finally, an environment may provide a consistent set of peers who become known over a period of time, or it may present a constantly changing assemblage of peers (Searcy & Meadows, 1994).

Families that move frequently may give their children an advantage in establishing peer relationships. Highly mobile children tend to have more friends than less mobile children do. This may be due in part to the fact that frequent movers are often more gregarious and tend to participate in more group activities, such as team sports.

A friend in the neighborhood who is also a school friend is likely to be more influential than a friend known only at school. Adolescents place a premium on friendships with school friends that extend to nonschool settings, relative to friends known only at school. Almost four-fifths reported that it was true (41%) or mostly true (37%) that they felt closer to school friends with whom they spent a lot of time outside of school. A similar proportion (77%) indicated that they knew more about school friends whom they saw frequently outside school (Belle, 1989).

Evidence suggests that quantity alone can be an issue. Children with a larger number of same-age peers in their networks tended to receive higher academic and behavior ratings from their teachers throughout the school year (Salzinger et al., 1988). Problems in friendships are often part of a broader syndrome of poor adjustment (Berndt & Savin-Williams, 1993). For example, students with behavior disorders spend more time in solitary play and less time interacting socially with their peers

(Searcy & Meadows, 1994).

In structuring social network interventions for a child, it is essential that clinicians obtain as much information as possible about the child's peer relations. Understanding the general characteristics and reputations of the child's friends is important in developing appropriately focused, effective intervention programs (Henggeler, 1991). Teachers, parents, and the child herself are often useful sources of this information. However, parents may not be reliable sources of information about their children's friends: Cochran and his colleagues (1990) found that when parents reported the presence of just one dependable friend, the child was likely to report friendship with two or more children or membership in a small clique.

Although information gathered from others is useful, it is no substitute for direct observation and assessment of peer relations. The clinician should arrange to have one or more informal meetings with the child and his or her peers. These informal gatherings can take various forms, from playing a pick-up basketball game or video games to going shopping. If it is impossible to arrange such an activity to coincide with the assessment, the clinician should catch the peer group for an informal exchange whenever they are usually together (e.g., after school at a fast food restaurant). Such meetings can provide considerable information regarding the antisocial/prosocial nature of the peer group as well as qualitative aspects of the child's peer relations (e.g., leader vs. follower, shy vs. assertive). In fact, meeting with the child's peer group is always advisable, even when the antisocial/prosocial tendencies of the peer group are already known (Henggeler, 1991).

Antisocial Behavior and Peers

Despite all the benefits of strong peer relationships, many parents of teenagers are concerned about the other side of the coin—the potentially bad influences of hanging out with the wrong crowd. Professionals share similar concerns about the types of people that children, especially adolescents, tend to associate with. A frequent goal of social system intervention is to decrease the child's involvement with deviant peers and to increase his or her association with prosocial peers (Henggeler, 1991).

If a youth is embedded in a deviant peer group (e.g., friends who have failing grades, engage in illegal activities, have little contact with prosocial activities, and/or have parents who provide little structure and monitoring), it may be necessary to remove the child from that peer group and to establish a new, more socially appropriate network of peers. However, because peer friendships are extremely important to adolescents, it is not advisable to sever peer relations unless these friendships are, without a doubt, directly linked with the child's behavior problems (Henggeler, 1991). This direct connection can be difficult to document, particularly when the information regarding the child's peers is contradictory. This is why the interventionist must spend the necessary time in the assessment phase gathering all possible information from sources both outside and inside the child's peer group.

Parents and professionals alike must recognize that associating with peers whose behavior is undesirable or antisocial is a popular way for teenagers to rebel. Adolescents can also be pushed toward such relationships through parenting mistakes or inadequacies. When parents are either negligent or inept in monitoring and disciplining teenage children, the children are not likely to develop good social skills, and they are more likely to form antisocial attitudes. Conformity to friends who encourage antisocial behavior peaks around 15 years of age, or the ninth grade of school (Berndt & Savin-Williams, 1993).

Parents are often quick to blame the child's friends for leading their child toward deviant or illicit behavior. The reality may be that their adolescent had already been using drugs (or whatever the behavior might be) for some time, and merely became friendly with a group of peers who also used them. Kandel (cited in Berndt & Savin-Williams, 1993) determined that increases in friends' similarity during the year was due about as much to friendship selection as to friends' influence. Thus, friends do not always deserve the blame they receive for an adolescent's behavior problems.

Interventions may be designed explicitly to select, modify, or structure the child's physical and/or social environment for the purpose of enhancing peer relationships. Parents, as managers of their children's social lives, are typically the facilitators of these types of influences. This managerial role involves performing two broad sets of activities. First, parents serve as arrangers of opportunities for peer-to-peer interaction by providing safe neighborhoods, organizing play groups, and enrolling their children in activities involving other children. Second, parents are also facilitators of peer relationships when they directly monitor and supervise their children's interactions with peers in order to facilitate the development of their children's social skills (Belle, 1989). The final sections of this chapter examine these alternative direct pathways by which families influence peer-to-peer interaction.

Parents as Facilitators of Peer Relationships

Parents play an important role in the facilitation of their children's peer relationships by initiating contact between their own children and potential "play" partners. Although this influence generally diminishes as a child gets older, it is critical for some children at certain stages of development, and it can have wide-ranging effects. For example, Belle (1989) found that school-age boys with parents who initiated peer contacts were better liked and less rejected by their classmates than were boys with non-initiating parents.

Parents can also have an effect by setting good examples. Evidence gathered by Searcy and Meadows (1994) reveals that a child's social networks are influenced by parents' own attitudes about friendships and the degree to which they model friendship skills and demonstrate the value of friends.

As professionals design intervention programs for children, they need to be aware of how the children's needs are being met (or are not being met) in the family. Some children will need more parental support in their peer relationships, whereas others will need increased autonomy from adults and greater access to peers. Parents must understand that school-age children need to spend some time with their peers in situations relatively free from adult supervision. The development of close same-sex friendships ("chums") in early adolescence, and the gradual development of opposite-sex relationships, are dependent on having adequate "free" time (Salzinger et al., 1988).

Interaction with school friends outside of school helps children establish and cement their peer networks in early adolescence. Parents can help by knowing who their children's school friends are and helping the group get together in other settings. Nonschool contact among friends can also be facilitated by encouraging teachers (as well as coaches, club leaders, etc.) to make assignments that involve students in out-of-school group activities.

Parental Monitoring and Supervision

During a child's adolescent stage, parents fill the role of monitor more often than that of facilitator. Monitoring is a composite measure of how well the parents keep track of their children's whereabouts, the kinds of companions they keep, and the types of activities they engage in. A number of studies of parental monitoring indicate that parents of delinquent children engage in less monitoring and supervision of their children's activities, especially with regard to children's use of evening time, than parents of nondelinquent children. Medrich and colleagues (1982) found that parents of delinquent sons tend to perceive themselves as being less in control of their sons' choice of friends.

A study of 7th- and 10th-grade boys found a significant correlation between lack of parental monitoring and court-reported delinquency, attacks against property, delinquent lifestyle, rule-breaking outside the home, and an antisocial disposition (characterized by fighting with peers, talking back to teachers, breaking school rules, etc.). Steinberg (cited in Parke & Kellam, 1994) found that children in the sixth through ninth grades, especially girls who are on their own after school, are more susceptible to peer pressure to engage in antisocial activity (e.g., vandalism, cheating, stealing) than are adult-supervised peers. Less well-monitored boys, regardless of the family's socioeconomic status, tend to receive lower grades in school and feel less competent at school-related activities than their peers who are monitored more closely.

Supervision can take many forms, and it does not have to be direct supervision to be effective. Adolescents who are at home after school without an adult present may be supervised distally by their parents through telephone calls, a prearranged and agreed-upon schedule that the adolescent is to follow, or the power of internalized parental controls, which may be heightened by the adolescent's being in his or her own house. There is evidence that distal monitoring can be effective; of adolescents who are on their own after school hours, those who are "hanging out" at a friend's house are generally more susceptible to peer pressure than adolescents who are on their own in their own homes. Further support for distal monitoring comes from the finding that adolescents whose parents know their whereabouts after school are less likely to be susceptible to peer pressure.

The importance of monitoring varies with other aspects of the family environment, including child-rearing practices. Steinberg (cited in Parke & Kellam, 1994) found that monitoring may be more important for some families than for others; specifically, children of parents who tend to use authoritative parenting practices were more susceptible to peer pressure in the absence of monitoring than children of parents whose child-rearing methods were less authoritative.

Attempts to gauge the effects of monitoring on behavior must take into account other conditions or variables that alter the impact of monitoring. For instance, developmental shifts may be important, since younger children are less likely to be left unsupervised than older children. Moreover, it is likely that direct supervision is more common among parents of younger children, whereas distal supervision is more evident among adolescents' parents.

A Final Caveat

Because variations in friends' support depend partly on children's personal characteristics, interventions that focus solely on changes in the social environment are shortsighted. Some children who do not have supportive friendships may need not only a supportive environment, but also training in the skills that are necessary for forming and maintaining friendships. Although current theories do not clearly identify the skills needed for obtaining support from friends, both the basic skills needed for participating in social relationships and the more specialized skills needed for seeking particular types of support from friends may be important.

It is also important to remember that it is impossible to make all of a child's social environments supportive. Children will adapt most successfully if they can form supportive friendships in a wide range of environments. Yet no child is so resilient that he or she can thrive in a completely unsupportive environment. Therefore, environmental change may be an essential element of a successful intervention. Changes in environments should be designed to increase children's chances of obtaining the type of support from friends that they need to cope with the stressors in their environments (Belle, 1988).

In conclusion, peer friendships are in large measure contextually driven. Friendships depend on opportunity and are difficult to develop without a supportive environment. Since children with behavior disorders are reported as having fewer peer interactions and more time spent alone, and by definition have a difficult time building and maintaining relationships, assessing how environments impact their relationships seems an important agenda. It would appear most pragmatic to encourage parents and teachers to create social structures that help children bridge their different environments, thereby strengthening friendships through common experiences across these shared settings (Searcy & Meadows, 1994).

9 Case Studies in Environmental Intervention

Chapter Preview
- Presents 4 examples of ecological case planning, with visual summaries

The four synopses of case planning in this chapter represent actual courses of ecological decision-making. The vignettes are intended to convey the essential flavor of environmental tactics rather than to illustrate all possibilities of analysis and intervention. In most cases, traditional counseling methods are used in conjunction with environmental approaches. The figures which accompany each case visually illustrate the intervention steps, with the letters corresponding to the descriptions in the text.

Henry: Male, Age 14

Diagnosis: Antisocial Behavior (including history of substance abuse and running away)

Problems: Henry acts out in school to get attention. He lives in a single-parent home with his mother and sister. The local community has many temptations for drug and alcohol use. He has a long history of frequent institutional placement for aggressive conduct disorder.

Goals: Maintain tight supervision of Henry in school and home environments. Help Henry express feelings constructively through activities.

Strategies: Place Henry in a specialized foster care setting and provide school day treatment. Also, outline structured daily activities with the foster family, and keep Henry isolated from his "delinquent" environment.

Comments:
A. Ecological approaches, emphasizing environmental modification, can be quite useful with conduct problems that have resisted traditional treatments.
B. An Environmental Status Exam revealed that Henry was intent on disrupting (and hence, controlling) any environment he entered. He had failed in half a dozen residential placements.
C. Henry and his family are hostile toward "psychotherapy" because of its previous failure. The mother has retained a lawyer to consider suing the state, forcing it to provide "appropriate" services for Henry.
D. Henry was placed in a school day treatment program with nine other students and a staff-to-student ratio of 1:2. The program, located in a small, renovated house on the campus of another school, stressed the teaching of social skills and utilized a reward system. The location facilitates acceptance of the program as "just another school."
E. Henry enrolled in a once-a-week Tae Kwon Do class that teaches discipline and philosophical aspects of the sport in addition to the physical routines.
F. Henry visits his mother and sister regularly. The mother's boyfriend attends twice-monthly counseling to receive guidance in how he can be helpful to Henry.
G. Henry has difficulty staying on task with any activity. The foster father is skilled in carpentry, and he involves Henry in some local building projects, slowly increasing the time commitment. Henry uses his earnings to purchase favorite CDs.
H. In the past, Henry has run away from any placement. Therefore, arrangements were made to secure specialized foster parents on a nearby island, accessible only by boat. The island, which cur-

Case Studies in Environmental Intervention   167

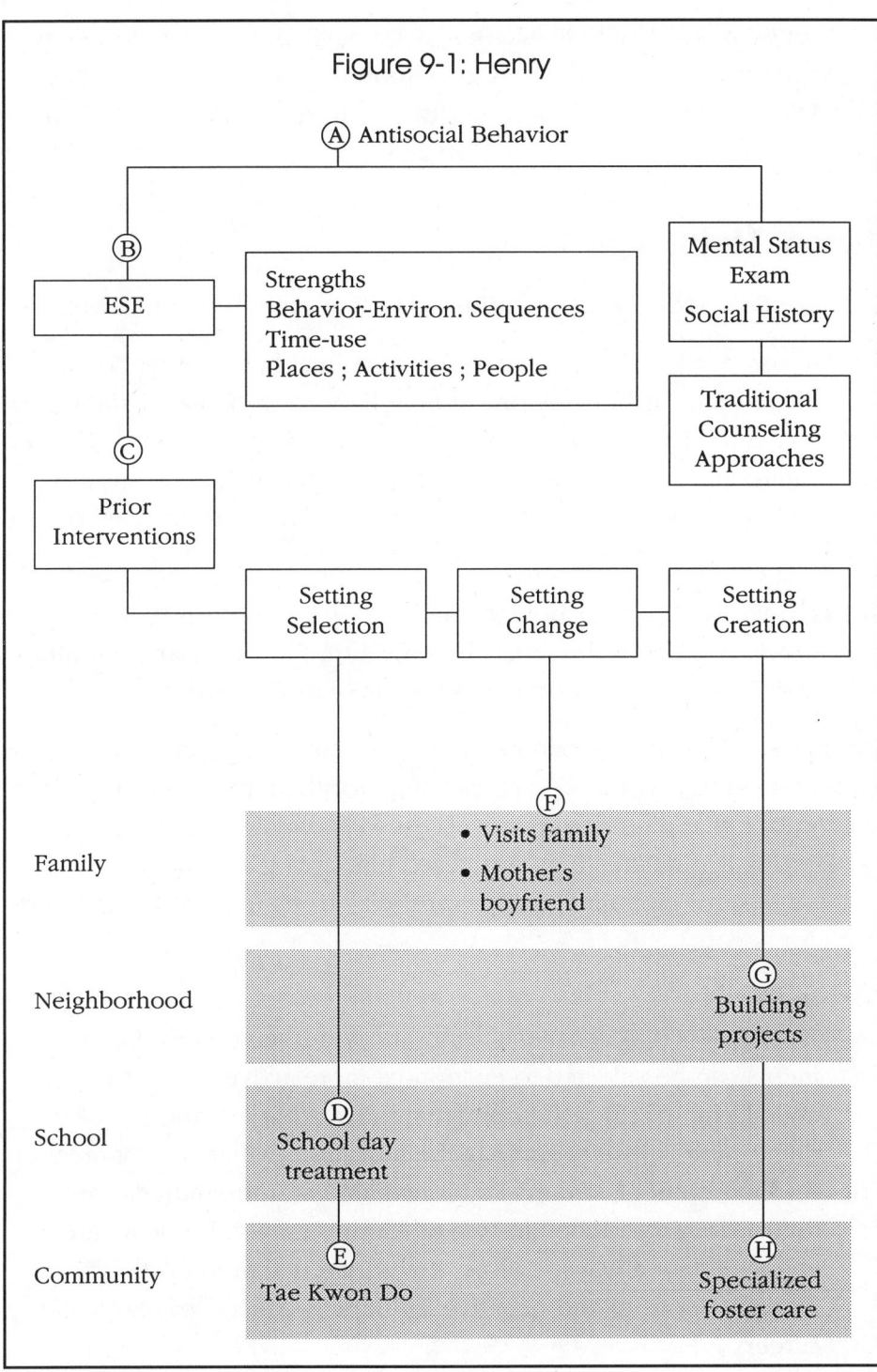

rently has about 100 residents, is going through a development phase, so new building projects abound. Specialized foster care in this location and the other efforts noted above allowed for Henry to be under supervision 24 hours a day, 7 days a week.

Aaron: Male, Age 11

Diagnosis: Childhood Depression (including social unresponsiveness)

Problems: Aaron has no friends. He gets into fights at school when other boys pick on him. Aaron's family lives in an isolated rural area with no nearby neighbors. The father is often away from home (for up to 6 months at a time) due to a job in the military. The family has moved frequently because of the father's career. Aaron receives poor grades in school.

Goals: Teach the parents how the military career controls their lifestyle and how to mediate its influence. Involve Aaron in a regular community activity. Increase the supportiveness of his school environment.

Strategies: Educate the parents on environmental influences, perhaps leading them to consider a career change for the father and/or moving to a location that provides greater access to playmates. Engage Aaron in weekly Boy Scouts meetings, and teach him how to make friends. Consult with school personnel and assist their efforts in facilitating friendships for Aaron.

Comments:
A. Depression is very amenable to lifestyle intervention. Environments can be selected to encourage more active behaviors. If a child lacks specific environmental skills, adult members of a setting can be enlisted to help in the transition to that environment.
B. An Environmental Status Exam revealed that the father's career totally dominated the lifestyle of Aaron's family. While a career change is not always realistic, environmental modifications can mediate some of the negative influences caused by particular careers.

Case Studies in Environmental Intervention 169

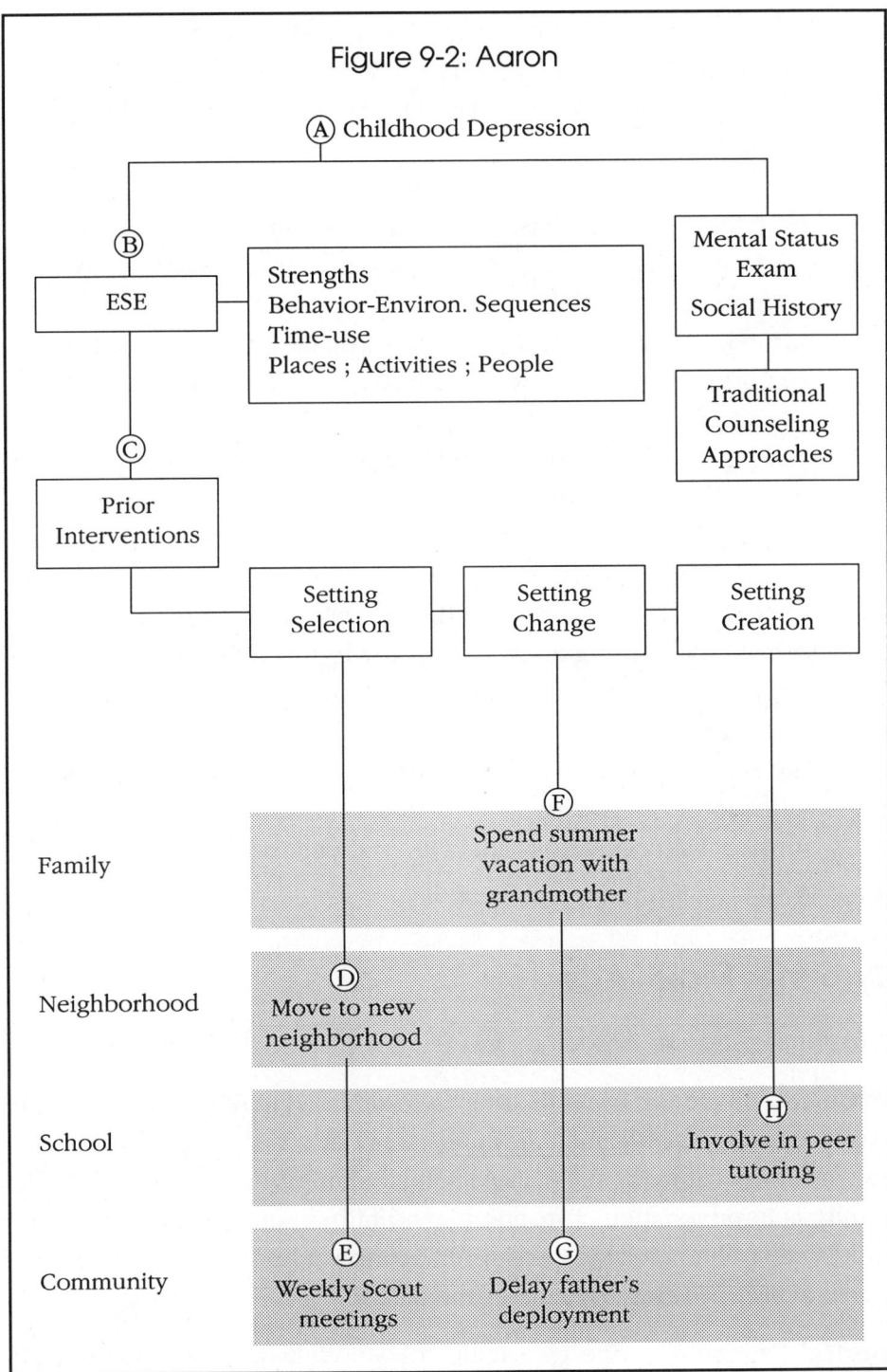

C. The father was already considering a career change. The family was "comfortable" with the child receiving weekly counseling sessions as the treatment. The family had a history of living in isolated rural areas.
D. The family began making arrangements to move to housing near the father's military base. The environment included access to children in Aaron's age range and opportunities for family involvement with others.
E. Aaron began attending weekly scout meetings. The scoutmaster was briefed on the child's circumstances and made special efforts to help.
F. Aaron had not been depressed in the past when the family lived in another state near his grandparents. When summer approached, arrangements were made for him to spend the summer months with his grandparents.
G. The father was to be deployed soon for another 6 months away from home. Arrangements were made through the military to delay the deployment so the father could continue in the family counseling.
H. The school guidance office set up a peer tutoring arrangement with another boy, who not only was a potential friend for Aaron, but also was relatively weak in an academic area that was one of Aaron's strengths.

Tyronne: Male, Age 15

Diagnosis: School Misbehavior (including history of school refusal)

Problems: Tyronne has little interest in school. He refuses to do homework and chores at home. He fights easily at school when bullied. He recently was cut from the school football team due to poor grades. The family is impoverished. Tyronne has no father, and his mother, who is mildly retarded, is unable to control Tyronne at home. There is a Family Court action pending because of the truancy.

Goals: Expose Tyronne to a male role model. Improve his mother's

Case Studies in Environmental Intervention

sense of control over the situation. Get Tyronne re-involved in a motivational school activity. Link the family with community services. Reestablish regular school attendance.

Strategies: Link the mother with a caseworker at the welfare department in order to obtain food stamps. Teach the mother a simple reward method designed to get Tyronne's cooperation with household chores. Investigate the circumstances of Tyronne's dismissal from football team and, if possible, try to get him reinstated. Enlist Tyronne's 22-year-old cousin, who lives nearby, to spend time with Tyronne and to provide a positive male image. Establish a liaison with the Family Court to provide support with the legal problem. Open a line of communication between the home and the school, so attendance can be checked on a daily basis.

Comments:
A. School misbehavior involves intervention on all ecological levels rather than only the educational setting.
B. The Environmental Status Exam revealed that Tyronne's equilibrium in the environment was upset by the loss of academic eligibility for football. His involvement in football had enabled him to function adequately at home and school.
C. The investigation into Tyronne's dismissal from the school football team revealed that it had resulted from his receiving a failing grade in only one subject. Subsequent testing revealed a previously undiscovered learning disability in that area. Tyronne was placed in a learning disabilities resource class for that subject.
D. The clinician established twice-monthly contact with Tyronne's probation officer. Also, the family was directly linked with a food stamp caseworker, who attended a counseling session and assisted the mother with the eligibility procedures.
E. The atmosphere of control at home was altered by teaching the mother a simple reward procedure. A small allowance, which Tyronne valued, was made contingent upon his accomplishing a list of household chores and compliance with a curfew.
F. Tyronne was allowed to rejoin the football team. Also, his school attendance was monitored directly by the clinician, who had daily

172 The Ecology of Troubled Children

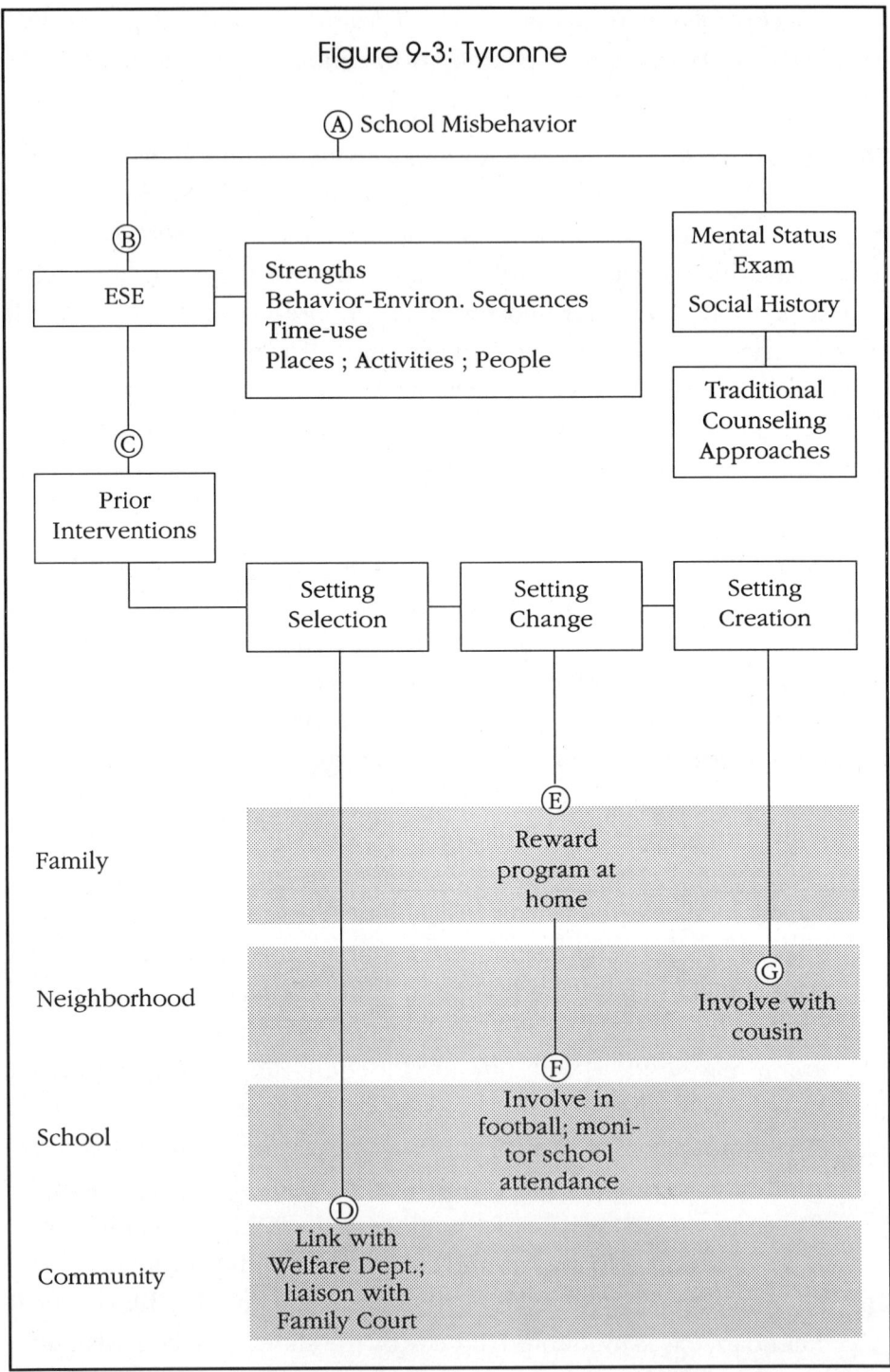

contact with the school.
G. The nearby cousin was enlisted to have regular contact with Tyronne. The cousin monitored Tyronne's progress and reported regularly to the clinician. He also usually planned a weekend activity with Tyronne.

Andrea: Female, Age 10

Diagnosis: Hyperactivity; at risk for child abuse

Problems: Andrea's mother is a single parent whose job requires overtime work. She feels completely exhausted and overwhelmed. The after-school child care being used is highly unreliable and causes frequent family disruptions. Andrea is aggressive with other children. She runs into traffic when not carefully supervised. Her mother is unable to follow through with behavior modification methods.

Goals: Provide respite care for Andrea's mother, reduce her stress load, and structure her lifestyle more realistically. Have the school institute a behavioral control method to transfer to the mother. Alter the mother's work circumstances to eliminate the overtime involvement. Involve Andrea in ongoing peer activities, and identify potential areas for her to experience success in school. Stabilize after-school child care.

Strategies: Conduct home visits to explore possible stress reductions in that setting. Hold a planning-linking conference that includes school personnel and a local minister. Enlist an after-school recreation program to provide peer activities for Andrea. Involve mother in weekly community activity to mobilize friendships. Institute a reward system to encourage positive behaviors.

Comments:
A. Environmental approaches help keep hyperactivity below a tolerance threshold. Parents who view medication as the only treatment option and resist traditional counseling may be more receptive to environmental kinds of intervention when these are used in conjunction with medication.

B. The Environmental Status Exam revealed many lifestyle stressors which could be potentially mediated by environmental adjustments. The mother spent most waking hours, except for work, with the child.
C. Andrea had been treated with traditional office therapy for over a year while living with her grandmother. The mother was desperate and on the verge of abusing the child.
D. The mother was encouraged to attend a weekly women's group at her neighborhood church. Child care was provided during these meetings. The mother also began attending Sunday services, where child care was also provided, offering another respite for her.
E. Andrea was enrolled in a neighboring school's after-school program, with bus transportation provided.
F. A home visit enabled the clinician to recommend adjustments in the household routines and physical environment of the home, further reducing stressors.
G. The mother successfully negotiated with her employer to reduce her workload.
H. Since the mother was resistant to weekly counseling sessions and had difficulty following through with behavior modification procedures, the school guidance counselor taught and monitored a reward program at a twice-monthly meeting with the mother. The meetings were viewed as a way to review the child's progress at school and, as a result, were less threatening to the mother.
I. The clinician monitored the various interventions by twice-monthly planning-linking conferences with the school counselor and the family minister.

Case Studies in Environmental Intervention 175

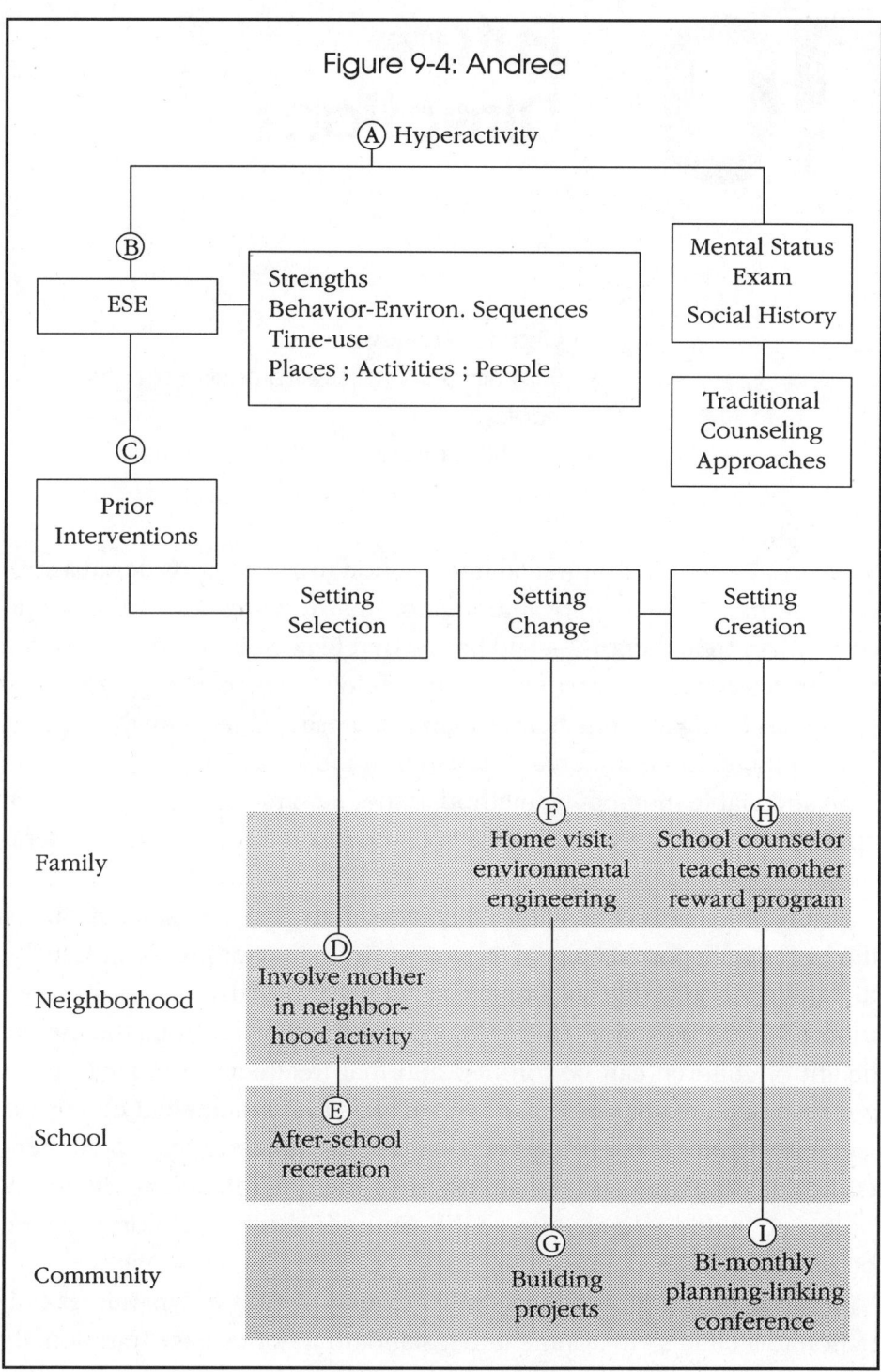

10 Future Directions

Chapter Preview
- Summarizes key issues in environmental ecology
- Identifies future directions in the field

Since the 1930s, environmental intervention has been considered a subordinate method—a minor intervention that requires less training and ability than "real therapy"—and has been relegated in some cases to the paraprofessional. Intervention into a child's environment is typically viewed as being less prestigious than the present clinical methods. This must change. Environmental intervention must gain status as a prominent and viable therapeutic method, rather than merely as an incidental effort that is relatively ineffectual in comparison to conventional therapies.

Henggeler (1991) has argued convincingly that a major reason for the historically poor results of treatments for behavior problems may be that the methods addressed only a small portion of the factors that contributed to the behavior. There is good reason to believe that the mental health of children can be fortified and that treatment efforts can meet with a much greater percentage of success if environmental ecology is given its rightful place in intervention. The weaknesses of present mental health programs and the strengths of the environmental viewpoint proposed in this volume point to the same conclusion—children will be better served by a change in the focus of mental health services.

Mental health professionals must extend the same dynamic examination to a child's environment that standard theories have traditionally accorded to individuals. With a broader conceptualization of practice, the environment becomes a strategic component of mental health's potential. But just how willing are mental health professionals to leave their offices and to face children's environments, especially in the reality of other community structures, reimbursement issues, and the comfort with business as usual? With the trend toward outreach services such as case management and in-home therapies, there is emerging optimism for change.

The systematic use of ecological knowledge is crucial in clinical practice, regardless of the disciplinary background, theoretical orientation, or personal comfort level of the practitioner. In some cases, environmental intervention could make direct psychological intervention unnecessary; in most cases it can serve as a valuable supplement. Furthermore, traditional treatment efforts can be made more permanent by targeting environmental supports—such as kin, friends, neighbors, and other informal helpers—who can help families sustain and consolidate the gains made in psychotherapy (Whittaker & Tracy, 1991). To take advantage of these environmental resources, mental health clinicians must be prepared to master much broader information and to grasp much more complex interactions than ever before. Many clinicians are now embracing this challenge.

The array of environmental strategies available to professionals can be compared to a cafeteria menu—various combinations of items can be selected or passed over and, if selected, can be taken in whatever size portion is desired. Of course, not all combinations produce equally competent children; some "ingredients" in the mix are more important to the healthy development of a child than others. Also, no one combination will be equally effective for all children; behavioral adaptations can be achieved through multiple pathways (Parke & Kellam, 1994).

Environmental intervention is not being advanced as the panacea for all the current problems and weaknesses in the field of mental health therapy. As with all mental health intervention strategies, there are inherent limitations in the environmental ecology orientation. It is important to acknowledge that some child behavior problems do have a neurological, medical, and/or educational basis. Such things as learning differences, and even disabilities, unquestionably exist (O'Callaghan, 1993). Unfortunately, although there is an expanding literature base on environmental intervention (Munger, 1991), there remains a dearth of ecological research about scientific correlations between individual problems and specific environmental factors.

One problem in implementing highly flexible, individualized intervention models is that, by definition, they require creativity in the design and implementation of treatment plans. The problems involved in replicating approaches that have flexibility as a hallmark are obvious (Melton, 1995). A shift toward an environmental approach to mental health intervention requires a corresponding shift away from reliance on specific treatment models and toward more generalized strategies, with the unique particulars filled in as the case develops. The cost of such customized programs can be measured in the up-front time commitment required of the clinician. The payoff is in greater effectiveness and duration of benefits for the client. Increasingly, mental health managed care has come to dominate the field. Its concomitant emphasis on effective outcomes is likely to encourage new methods which clinicians must master. Further, the CASSP system of care model continues toward widespread adoption throughout the United States. Both of these phenomena are consistent with the environmental viewpoint. So, in the next decade, as professionals look to spend less time in direct treatment of children and more time working through the environment, clinical environmental ecology is likely to enter the mainstream as a foundation for intervention design.

Glossary

Behavior setting. A combination of a specific place, a specific time, and a standing pattern of behavior (Russell & Ward, 1982).

Competence. Effective functioning within one's environment (Goldfried & D'Zurilla, 1969).

Competence-oriented intervention. Mental health treatment that emphasizes understanding the environment, with all its complexities, and restructuring it in a purposeful and systematic fashion. Intervention activities may be directed toward the physical environment, the social milieu, or both. Often, a person's environment needs to be modified or restructured to facilitate or support his or her coping efforts (Maluccio, 1981).

Cultural relativity. The idea that acceptable behavior varies depending on a culture's particular norms. Proponents of the ecological model agree that in order for a behavior to be considered disturbing, a concerned adult must identify it as such, and that the standards that define what is disturbing are culturally relative (Swap, 1984).

Developmental trajectory. The persisting patterns of motivation and activity that a particular environment induces in individuals (Bronfenbrenner, 1979).

Deviance. A quality that lies not in a behavior itself, but in the interaction between the person who commits an act and those who respond to it (Becker, 1976).

Ecological. Relating to the way an organism and its immediate environment (the "ecological niche") respond to each other. In the context of child behavior, an ecological perspective proposes that we cannot account for or understand the intimate relationships between a child and the child's parents without understanding how the conditions surrounding the family affect family interactions and define the family's particular experience. The most important thing about this ecological perspective is that it reveals connections that might otherwise go unnoticed; it helps us look beyond the immediate and the obvious to see where the most significant influences lie (Garbarino, 1982).

Ecological environment. A nested arrangement of structures (each structure contained within the next) which comprise the environment: microsystem, mesosystem, exosystem, and macrosystem (Bronfenbrenner, 1979).

Ecological therapist. One who alters transactions between individuals and their environments in a manner that helps optimize the present as well as the future psychosocial functioning of the individuals (Henggeler, 1982).

Ecologists. Scientists who study the pattern of relationships between organisms and their environments (McConnell, 1977).

Ecology. A branch of biology that deals with the relation of living things to their environment and to each other. Applied to humans, ecology is concerned with maximizing fit (and reducing discord) between people and their environments (Jeger & Slotnick, 1982).

Eco-map. An assessment and intervention tool that uses a graphic representation to map the ecological system, the boundaries of which encompass the person or family in the life-space. Included in the map are the major systems that are parts of the family's life and the nature of the family's relationships with the various systems (Hartman, cited in Swap, 1984).

Ecosystem. A geographical area and the things that live there (Catalano, 1979). For human ecologists, the term refers to the person or community of people being studied, together with the natural habitat (Feagans, 1974).

Embeddedness. The condition of being embedded in (and influenced by) a surrounding set of events (Cohen, Evans, Stokols, & Krantz, 1986).

Environment. Everything outside an organism. A child's environment is composed of three components—physical milieu, human components, and the existing formal and informal patterns of behavior (Gump, 1980). For example, the developing child's environment includes family, friends, neighborhood, and school, as well as less immediate forces such as laws, social attitudes, and institutions that directly or indirectly affect the child (Garbarino, 1982).

Environmental competence. A combination of two factors: awareness of the environment and its influence on efforts to reach goals and meet needs, and the ability to decide what environmental changes are necessary to intervene effectively (Germain, 1981).

Environmental engineering. Matching a set of objectives for a particular person with an environment that will facilitate the attainment of those objectives (Bloom, 1984).

Environmental inertia. The properties of a system which create a momentum of its own toward particular behaviors; it is caused by the specific relation between the person and environment (Bronfenbrenner, 1979).

Environmental press. The combined influence of forces working in a particular setting to shape the behavior and development of individuals in that setting. Environmental press arises from circumstances confronting and surrounding an individual that generate psychosocial momentum tending to guide that individual in a particular direction (Garbarino, 1982).

Environmental psychology. The branch of psychology concerned with providing a systematic account of the relationship between people and their physical environments (Russell & Ward, 1982).

Environmental reconnaissance. Observation and investigation of environmental attributes (Vincent & Trickett, 1983).

Environmental repertoire. The provision of environmental resources and opportunities that will enable a person to engage in a broader array of behaviors, or choose from a greater number of alternatives, thereby increasing his or her freedom (Jeger & Slotnick, 1982).

Environmental Status Exam (ESE). One of the first steps in ecological intervention, the ESE involves two steps: (1) identifying sources of discord in the ecosystem and sources of support that can be used to improve the goodness of fit between an individual and important people and places in his or her life, and (2) specifying what supports are required to enable the person to make reasonable progress toward achievable developmental goals (Hobbs, cited in Cook & Plas, 1984).

Environmental trajectories. The predictable influence of particular settings on behavior, due not to the internal properties of the settings themselves but to the position of the settings in the larger context of meso-, exo-, and macrosystems (Bronfenbrenner, 1979).

Exosystem. An extension of the mesosystem embracing other specific social structures, both formal and informal, that do not themselves contain the developing person but impinge upon or encompass the person's immediate settings, and thereby influence or even determine what goes on there. These structures include the major institutions of the society, both deliberately structured and spontaneously evolving, as they operate at a concrete local level (Bronfenbrenner, 1979).

Family. A term commonly used to refer to all the people in one household, whether related by blood or not (Pattison, 1981).

Goodness of fit. The congruence (match) between an organism's individual characteristics and the environment in which it is placed (Apter, 1982).

Habitat. The social and physical environment in which an organism lives (Morse, Smith, & Acker, 1978).

Indirect influence. The process whereby an agent or physical event influences another agent or event through the mediation of a third person, object, or event (Parke, 1978).

Individual differences. The wide variations in people's behavior, which must be taken into account when evaluating a given system. The person alone is not a good predictor of future behavior; neither is the environment alone. The interaction between the person and the environment is the important factor (Apter, 1982).

Intervener. An equivalent term for "therapist," but encompassing a new model rather than the old "healer" model. The former "patient" is redefined as a person behaving in a maladaptive manner that is both personally unsatisfying and disruptive or disturbing to at least one group of close family, friends, or associates. Instead of using pathology as an index, interveners are concerned with degrees of distress and predicaments (Pattison, 1981).

Kin. Those bound by birth or marriage (Caplan, 1974).

Life domains. Different spheres of an individual's life, such as family, education, spiritual activities, recreation, employment, etc. (Cohen, Evans, Stokols, & Krantz, 1986).

Life-space. The momentary situation or surrounding pattern of forces in a particular place (Apter & Conoley, 1984).

Life-space structures. The characteristic ways an individual organizes the key resources in his or her life—time, space, people, and activity (Lee, 1985).

Macrosystem. The complex of overarching institutional patterns of the culture or subculture—such as the economic, social, educational, legal, and political systems—of which micro-, meso-, and exosystems are the concrete manifestations (Bronfenbrenner, 1979).

Manning theory. A theory pertaining to the number of people in a particular environment and the behavioral options inherent in that environment. Undermanned environments have too few people relative to the number of behavior settings; overmanned environments have too many people relative to the number of available behavior settings (Jeger & Slotnick, 1982).

Mental health. Mental health consists of being able to function successfully in terms of one's own goals, abilities, and opportunities within the context of one's social and physical environment (Ringness, cited in Apter, 1982).

Mesosystem. The interrelations among major settings containing the developing person at a particular point in his or her life. A mesosystem is a system of microsystems (Bronfenbrenner, 1979).

Microsystem. The complex of relations between a developing person and the environment in an immediate setting containing that person (e.g., home, school, work) (Bronfenbrenner, 1979).

Mutual aid group. A group composed of peers who have convened voluntarily to offer face-to-face mutual help in solving a common problem or meeting a common need (Gottlieb, 1983).

Natural caregivers. Persons whose work roles bring them into repeated contact with large numbers of citizens who come to trust them and open up to them about their problems and worries. Family physicians, divorce lawyers, the clergy, and teachers are examples (Gottlieb, 1981).

Natural helper. A person such as a grocer, neighbor, spouse, friend, and so on, to whom, because of the person's concern, interest, and "innate" understanding, people "naturally" turn for help (Collins & Pancoast, 1976).

Natural support system. The set of presently significant others who are either members of one's social network, e.g., family and friends, or affiliated non-mental-health professionals, e.g., physicians and clergy (Hirsh, 1980).

Negative network orientation. The expectation or belief that it is inadvisable, impossible, useless, or potentially dangerous to draw on network resources (Tolsdorf, 1976).

Network. All or some of the social units (individuals or groups) with which a particular individual or group is in contact (Bott, cited in Tolsdorf, 1976).

Network orientation. A set of beliefs, attitudes, and expectations concerning the potential usefulness of a person's network members in helping him or her cope with a problem (Tolsdorf, cited in Vaux, Burda, & Stewart, 1986).

Network therapy. An intervention designed to reestablish the social network as a functioning unit, so that its members become closer and more involved with one another in a new and revitalized manner (Schoenfeld, 1984).

Niche. A place or activity for which a person is best fitted, or a habitat supplying the factors necessary for the existence of organisms.

Normative behavior. Behaviors that are within the range of acceptability as defined by the culture (Morse, Smith, & Acker, 1978).

Observer attribution bias. The tendency of an observer to overestimate the role of dispositional factors in influencing a person's behavior. The observer is more likely to make dispositional attributions than situational attributions about a person's behavior, since situational cues are often hidden, weak, or unknown.

Optimal environments. Those environments that maximize the fulfillment of a person's needs and the accomplishment of his or her goals and plans (Stokols, 1977).

Personality. A small and distinct group of primary traits in an individual that persist and endure, exhibiting a high degree of consistency across situations (Millon, 1981).

Planning-linking conference. A meeting consisting of a patient/client, significant others from folk-support systems, case managers, and selected providers with the greatest knowledge of the patient/client (Joint Commission on Hospital Accreditation, cited in Cutler & Madore, 1980).

Positive network orientation. A set of beliefs or expectations held by a person that it is safe, advisable, and, in some cases, necessary to confide in the social network and draw on it for advice, support, and feedback in stressful situations (Tolsdorf, 1976).

Progressive conformity. The tendency of people to become more like their environments—i.e., more like the majority of the other people in their milieus (Moos, 1976).

Ripple effect principle. Stemming from the assumption that all systems are interactive and interdependent (i.e., everything is connected to everything else), this principle holds that if change occurs in one part of a system, its effect will be felt in all other parts of the system. Similarly, if change occurs in one system, it is likely to affect contiguous systems (Grinnell, Kyte, & Bostwick, 1981).

Second-order linkages. Relationships consisting of people who are not in direct contact with a client but who are linked to members of the client's network (Cohen & Adler, 1986).

Self-help group. Voluntary, small-group structures established for mutual aid and the accomplishment of a special purpose. They are usually formed by peers who have come together for mutual assistance in satisfying a common need or overcoming a common deficit or life-disruption problem, and bringing about specific desired social and/or personal changes (Katz & Bender, cited in Jeger, Slotnick, & Shure, 1982).

Settings. Geographic locations in which various personal or interpersonal situations recur on a regular basis (Cohen, Evans, Stokols, & Krantz, 1986).

Social ecology. The multidisciplinary study of the impacts that physical and social environments have on human beings. Its primary concern is with the assessment and optimization of human milieus (Moos, 1975).

Social network. The people with whom an individual normally interacts on a face-to-face basis, including social intimates such as nuclear family members and close friends, as well as more socially distant persons such as neighbors, co-workers, and extended family members (Gottlieb, 1983).

Social support. Interpersonal transactions that include one or more of the following key elements: positive affect, affirmation, and aid (Kahn & Antonucci, 1980).

Social support network. A set of interconnected people that provides enduring patterns of nurturance (in any or all forms) and provides contingent reinforcement for efforts to cope with life on a day-to-day basis (Richardson & Pfeiffenberger, 1983).

Support. Any action or behavior that functions to assist the focal person in meeting his or her personal goals or in dealing with the demands of a particular situation (Tolsdorf, 1976).

Support systems. An individual, network, group, or organization whose continuing interactions with an individual provide him or her with opportunities to receive feedback about themselves and validation of their expectations about others. Such interactions may offset deficiencies in these communications within the larger community context (Caplan, 1976).

Therapeutic case advocacy. An intervention approach that attempts to change elements of the environment so as to accommodate a child's disability. The primary goal of therapeutic case advocacy is to organize or modify the behavior settings that constitute a child's environment so that together they can function as a system of care (Young, 1990).

References

Apter, S. (1982). *Troubled children/troubled systems.* Elmsford, NY: Pergamon.

Apter, S., & Conoley, J. (1984). *Childhood behavior disorders and emotional disturbance.* Englewood Cliffs, NJ: Prentice-Hall.

Asp, E., & Garbarino, J. (1983). Social support networks and the schools. In J. Whittaker & J. Garbarino (Eds.), *Social support networks: Informal helping in the human services* (pp. 251-297). New York: Aldine.

Bachman, J. (1987, July). An eye on the future. *Psychology Today,* pp. 6, 8.

Barker, R. (1968). *Ecological psychology: Concepts and methods for studying the environment of human behavior.* Palo Alto, CA: Stanford University Press.

Barker, R., & Gump, P. (1964). *Big school, small school: High school size and student behavior.* Palo Alto, CA: Stanford University Press.

Bass, C. (1985). Running can modify classroom behavior. *Journal of Learning Disabilities, 3,* 160-161.

Bechtel, R. (1984). Patient and community: The ecological bond. In W. O'Connor & B. Lubin (Eds.), *Ecological approaches in clinical and community psychology* (pp. 216-231). New York: Wiley.

Becker, H. (1976). On labeling outsiders. In A. Dean, A. Kraft, & B. Pepper (Eds.), *The social setting of mental health* (pp. 218-223). New York: Basic Books.

Becvar, R., Becvar, D., & Bender, A. (1982). Let us first do no harm. *Journal of Marital and Family Therapy, 8,* 385-391.

Behar, L., Zipper, I., & Weil, M. (1994). *Case management for children's mental health: A training curriculum for child-serving agencies.* Raleigh, NC: North Carolina Division of MH/DD/SAS.

Belle, D. (Ed.). (1989). *Children's social networks and social supports.* New York: Wiley.

Bennett, T., Lingerfelt, B., & Nelson, D. (1990). *Developing individualized family support plans: A training manual.* Cambridge, MA: Brookline Books.

Benson, P. (1991). *The troubled journey: A profile of American youth.* Minneapolis, MN: Lutheran Brotherhood.

Berndt, T., & Savin-Williams, R. (1993). Peer relations and friendships. In P. Tolan & B. Cohler (Eds.), *Handbook of clinical research and practice with adolescents* (pp. 203-219). New York: Wiley.

Bess, S. (1994). *Nobody don't love nobody: Lessons on love from the school with no name.* Carson City, NV: Old Leaf Press.

References

Bloom, B. (1984). *Community mental health: A general introduction* (2nd ed.). Monterey, CA: Brooks/Cole.

Bogenschneider, K., Small, S., & Riley, D. (1990, September). *An ecological risk-focused approach for addressing youth-at-risk issues.* Paper presented at the Youth At Risk Summit of the National Extension Service, Washington, D.C.

Bredemeir, B., Weiss, M., Shields, D., & Cooper, B. (1986). The relationship of sport involvement with children's moral reasoning and aggression tendencies. *Journal of Sport Psychology, 8,* 304-318.

Bronfenbrenner, U. (1979). *The ecology of human development.* Cambridge, MA: Harvard University Press.

Browne, B., & Francis, S. (1993). Participants in school-sponsored and independent sports: Perceptions of self and family. *Adolescence, 28,* 383-391.

Burchard, J., & Clarke, R. (1990). The role of individualized care in a service delivery system for children and adolescents with severely maladjusted behavior. *Journal of Mental Health Administration, 17,* 48-60.

Burchard, J., Burchard, S., Sewell, R., & VanDenBerg, J. (1993). *One kid at a time: Evaluative case studies and description of the Alaska youth initiative demonstration project.* Washington, DC: CASSP Technical Assistance Center.

Caplan, G. (1974). *Support systems and community mental health.* New York: Human Sciences Press.

Caplan, G. (1976). The family as support system. In G. Caplan & M. Killilea (Eds.), *Support systems and mutual help* (pp. 19-36). New York: Grune & Stratton.

Carnegie Council on Adolescent Development. (1992). *A matter of time: Risk and opportunity in the nonschool hours.* New York: Carnegie Corporation.

Catalano, R. (1979). *Health, behavior, and the community: An ecological perspective.* New York: Pergamon.

Clark, R. (1988). *Critical factors in why disadvantaged students succeed or fail in school.* New York: Academy for Educational Development.

Clark, T., Zalis, T., & Sacco, F. (1982). *Outreach family therapy.* New York: Jason Aronson.

Cochran, M. (1993). Parenting and personal social networks. In T. Luster & L. Okagaki (Eds.), *Parenting: An ecological perspective* (pp. 149-178). Hillsdale, NJ: Erlbaum.

Cochran, M., & Brassard, J. (1979). Child development and personal social networks. *Child Development, 50,* 601-616.

Cochran, M., Larner, M., Riley, D., Gunnarsson, L., & Henderson, C. (1990). *Extending families: The social networks of parents and their children.* New York: Cambridge University Press.

Cohen, C., & Adler, A. (1986). Assessing the role of social network interventions with an inner-city population. *American Journal of Orthopsychiatry, 56,* 278-288.

Cohen, S., Evans, G., Stokols, D., & Krantz, D. (1986). *Behavior, health, and environmental stress.* New York: Plenum.

Collins, A., & Pancoast, D. (1976). *Natural helping networks: A strategy for prevention.* Washington, D.C.: National Association of Social Workers.

Combrinck-Graham, L. (1990). *Giants*

steps: *Therapeutic innovations in child mental health*. New York: Basic Books.

Conyne, R., & Clark, R. (1981). *Environmental assessment and design*. New York: Praeger.

Cook, V., & Plas, P. (1984). Intervention with disturbed children: The ecological viewpoint. In M. Fine (Ed.), *Systematic intervention with disturbed children* (pp. 157-178). New York: Spectrum.

Csikszentmihalyi, M., & Larson, R. (1984). *Being adolescent: Conflict and growth in the teenage years*. New York: Basic Books.

Csikszentmihalyi, M., Rathunde, K., & Whalen, S. (1993). *Talented teenagers: The roots of success and failure*. New York: Cambridge University Press.

Cutler, D., & Madore, E. (1980). Community-family network therapy in a rural setting. *Community Mental Health Journal, 16,* 144-155.

DeAngelis, T. (1993). Support from neighbors, clergy no longer tapped. *APA Monitor, 24*(7), pp. 30-31.

Dunst, C., Trivette, C., & Deal, A. (1988). *Enabling and empowering families: Principles and guidelines for practice*. Cambridge, MA: Brookline Books.

Epstein, J., & Karweit, N. (Eds.). (1983). *Friends in school: Patterns of selection in secondary schools*. New York: Academic Press.

Erickson, J. (1988). *Directory of American youth organizations*. Minneapolis, MN: Free Spirit Publishing.

Family Services Research Center (1995). *Multisystemic therapy trainer's handbook*. Charleston, SC: Department of Psychiatry and Behavioral Sciences, Medical University of South Carolina.

Farbstein, J., & Kantrowitz, M. (1978). *People in places: Experiencing, using, and changing the built environment*. Englewood Cliffs, NJ: Prentice-Hall.

Feagans, L. (1974). Ecological theory as a model for constructing a theory of emotional disturbance. In W. Rhodes & M. Tracy (Eds.), *A study of child variance: Vol. 1. Conceptual models* (pp. 323-389). Ann Arbor, MI: University of Michigan Press.

Felner, R., Brand, S., Adan, A., Mulhall, P., Flowers, N., Sartain, B., & Dubois, D. (1993). Restructuring the ecology of the school as an approach to prevention during school transitions: Longitudinal follow-ups and extensions of the school transitional environment project (STEP). *Prevention in Human Services, 10,* 103-136.

Fine, M. (1992). A systems-ecological perspective on home-school intervention. In M. Fine & C. Carlson (Eds.), *The handbook of family-school intervention: A systems perspective* (1-17). Boston: Allyn and Bacon.

Fitzgerald, E., & Illback, R. (1993, March). *The measurement and effects of social support to families participating in Kentucky impact*. Paper presented at the 6th Annual Research Conference, "System of Care for Children's Mental Health: Building a Research Base," Research and Training Center for Children's Mental Health, Florida Mental Health Institute, Tampa.

Friedman, R. (1993). Preparation of students to work with children and families: Is it meeting the need? *Administration and Policy in Mental Health, 20,* 297-310.

Fulghum, R. (1988). *All I really need to know I learned in kindergarten: Un-*

common thoughts on common things. New York: Villard Books.

Garbarino, J. (1982). *Children and families in the social environment.* Chicago: Aldine.

Germain, C. (1981). The physical environment and social work practice. In A. Maluccio (Ed.), *Promoting competence in clients: A new/old approach to social work practice* (pp. 103-124). New York: The Free Press.

Garrison, J. (1981). Clinical construction of action social networks. *International Journal of Family Therapy, 3,* 258-267.

Gatti, F., & Colman, C. (1976). Community network therapy: An approach to aiding families with troubled children. *American Journal of Orthopsychiatry, 46,* 608-617.

Gavin, J. (1989, March). Your brand of sweat. *Psychology Today,* pp. 50-57.

Glassner, B., & Freedman, J. (1979). *Clinical sociology.* New York: Longman, Inc.

Goldberg, J. (1987, March 3). How four-footed friends help kids grow. *USA Today,* p. 6D.

Goldfried, M., & D'Zurilla, T. (1969). A behavioral-analytic model for assessing competence. In C. Speilberger (Ed.), *Current topics in clinical and community psychology: Vol. 1* (pp. 151-196). New York: Academic Press.

Goodhart, D., & Zautra, A. (1984). Assessing quality of life in the community: An ecological approach. In W. O'Connor & B. Lubin (Eds.), *Ecological approaches in clinical and community psychology* (pp. 251-292). New York: Wiley.

Gottlieb, B. (1981). Social networks and social support in community mental health. In B. Gottlieb (Ed.), *Social networks and social support* (pp. 11-39). Beverly Hills, CA: Sage.

Gottlieb, B. (1983). *Social support strategies: Guidelines for mental health practice.* Beverly Hills, CA: Sage.

Greenberger, E., & Steinberg, L. (1986). *When teenagers work: The psychological and social costs of adolescent employment.* New York: Basic Books.

Greenwood, C., Carta, J., & Hall, R. (1988). The use of peer tutoring strategies in classroom management and educational instruction. *School Psychology Review, 17,* 258-275.

Grinnell, R., Kyte, N., & Bostwick, G. (1981). Environmental modification. In A. Maluccio (Ed.), *Promoting competence in clients: A new/old approach to social work practice* (pp. 152-184). New York: The Free Press.

Gump, P. (1980). The school as a social situation. *Annual Review of Psychology, 31,* 553-582.

Gump, P. (1984). Ecological psychology and clinical mental health. In W. O'Connor & B. Lubin (Eds.), *Ecological approaches to clinical and community psychology* (pp. 57-71). New York: Wiley.

Haber, R. (1987). Friends in family therapy: Use of a neglected resource. *Family Process, 26,* 269-281.

Harari, O., & Hosey, K. (1981). Attributional biases among clinicians and non-clinicians. *Journal of Clinical Psychology, 37,* 445-450.

Hartman, L. (1978). Diagrammatic assessment of family relationships. *Social Casework, 59,* 465-476.

Hartman, L., & Laird, J. (1983). *Family-centered social work practice.* New York: The Free Press.

Heath, S., & McLaughlin, M. (1991).

Community organizations as family: Endeavors that engage and support adolescents. *Phi Delta Kappan, 20,* 623-627.

Heller, K., & Monahan, J. (1977). *Psychology and community change.* Homewood, IL: Dorsey Press.

Heller, K., & Swindle, R. (1983). Social networks, perceived social support, and coping with stress. In R. Felner, L. Jason, J. Moritsugu, & S. Farber (Eds.), *Preventive psychology* (pp. 87-103). New York: Pergamon.

Henderson, Z. (1987). Cognitive test scores tied to adult mentors. *Human Ecology Forum, 16,* 29.

Henggeler, S. (1982). The family-ecological systems theory. In S. Henggeler (Ed.), *Delinquency and adolescent psychopathology: A family-ecological systems approach* (pp. 1-10). Boston: John Wright.

Henggeler, S. (1991). *Treating conduct problems in children and adolescents: An overview of the multisystemic approach with guidelines for intervention design and implementation.* Columbia, SC: South Carolina Department of Mental Health.

Henggeler, S., & Borduin, C. (1990). *Family therapy and beyond: A multisystemic approach to treating the behavior problems of children and adolescents.* Pacific Grove, CA: Brooks-Cole.

Hirsh, B. (1980). Natural support systems and coping with major life changes. *American Journal of Community Psychology, 8,* 159-172.

Hobbs, N. (1982). *The troubled and troubling child.* San Francisco: Jossey-Bass.

Hollister, W., Edgerton, J., & Hunter, R. (1985). *Alternative services in community mental health: Programs and processes.* Chapel Hill, NC: University of North Carolina Press.

Ianni, F. (1989). *The search for structure: A report on American youth today.* New York: The Free Press.

Jason, L., Danner, K., & Kurasaki, K. (Eds.). (1993). Prevention and school transitions [Special issue]. *Prevention in Human Services, 10*(2).

Jeger, A., & Slotnick, R. (1982). Community mental health: Toward a behavioral-ecological perspective. In A. Jeger & R. Slotnick (Eds.), *Community mental health and behavioral-ecology* (pp. 7-26). New York: Plenum.

Jeger, A., Slotnick, R., & Shure, M. (1982). Toward a "self-help/professional collaborative perspective" in mental health. In D. Biegel & A. Naparstek (Eds.), *Community support systems and mental health: Research, practice, and policy* (pp. 205-223). New York: Springer.

Jones, E., & Nisbett, R. (1971). *The actor and observer: Divergent perceptions of the causes of behavior.* Morristown, NJ: General Learning Press.

Kahn, R., & Antonucci, T. (1980). Convoys across the life course: Attachment, roles, and social support. In P. Baltes & O. Brim (Eds.), *Life span development and behavior: Vol. 3* (pp. 253-286). New York: Academic Press.

Katz-Leavy, J., Lourie, I., Stroul, B., & Zeigler-Dendy, C. (1992). *Individualized services in a system of care.* Washington, DC: CASSP Technical Assistance Center.

Kerr, M., & Nelson, C. (1983). *Strategies*

References

for managing behavior problems in the classroom. Columbus, OH: Charles E. Merrill.

Kinney, J., Haapala, D., & Booth, C. (1991). *Keeping families together: The Homebuilders model*. Hawthorne, NY: Aldine de Gruyter.

Knitzer, J., Steinberg, Z., & Fleisch, B. (1990). *At the schoolhouse door: An examination of programs and policies for children with behavioral and emotional problems*. New York: Bank Street College of Education.

Kozol, J. (1974). *The night is dark and I am far from home*. Boston: Houghton Mifflin.

Kraft, S., & DeMaio, T. (1982). An ecological intervention with adolescents in low income families. *American Journal of Orthopsychiatry, 52*, 131-140.

Larson, R., & Richards, M. (Eds.). (1989). The changing life space of early adolescence [Special issue]. *Journal of Youth and Adolescence, 18*(6).

Larson, R., & Kleiber, D. (1993). Daily experience of adolescents. In P. Tolan & B. Cohler (Eds.), *Handbook of clinical research and practice with adolescents* (pp. 125-145). New York: Wiley.

Lee, M. (1985). *Life space structure: Explorations and speculations*. Human Relations, 38, 623-642.

Leff, H. (1978). *Experience, environments, and human potentials*. New York: Oxford University Press.

Lipsitz, J. (1986). *After school: Young adolescents on their own*. Carrboro, NC: Center for Early Adolescence.

Maguire, L. (1991). *Social support systems in practice: A generalist approach*. Silver Springs, MD: National Association of Social Workers.

Maluccio, A. (1981). Competence-oriented social work practice: An ecological approach. In A. Maluccio (Ed.), *Promoting competence in clients: A new/old approach to social work practice* (pp. 1-24). New York: The Free Press.

Mannino, F., & Shore, M. (1984). An ecological perspective on family intervention. In W. O'Connor & B. Lubin (Eds.), *Ecological approaches to clinical and community psychology* (pp. 75-93). New York: Wiley.

Martin, B. (1975). Parent-child relations. In F. Horowitz (Ed.), *Review of child development research: Vol. 4* (pp. 463-541). Chicago: University of Chicago Press.

McConnell, J. (1977). *Understanding human behavior* (2nd ed.). New York: Holt, Rinehart and Winston.

McGovern, M., Lyons, J., & Pomp, H. (1990). Capitation payment systems and pubic mental health care: Implications for psychotherapy with the seriously mentally ill. *American Journal of Orthopsychiatry, 60*, 298-304.

Medrich, E., Roizen, J., Rubin, V., & Buckley, S. (1982). *The serious business of growing up: A study of children's lives outside school*. Berkeley, CA: University of California Press.

Meer, J. (1986, May). The strife of bath. *Psychology Today*, p. 6.

Melton, G. (1995). Why don't the knuckleheads use common sense? In S. Henggeler & A. Santos (Eds.), *Innovative models of mental health treatment for "difficult to treat" clinical populations*. Washington, D.C.: American Psychiatric Press.

Milardo, R. (1988). *Families and social networks*. Newbury Park, CA: Sage.

Millon, T. (1981). *Disorders of person-*

ality: DSM III: Axis II. New York: Wiley.

Moos, R. (1975). Social ecology: Multidimensional studies of humans and human milieus. In S. Arieti (Ed.), *American handbook of psychiatry* (2nd ed.). (pp. 914-931). New York: Basic Books.

Moos, R. (1976). *The human context*. New York: Wiley.

Morse, W., Smith, J., & Acker, N. (1978). *Videotape training packages in child variance. The ecological approach: A self-instructional module*. Ann Arbor, MI: University of Michigan School of Education.

Munger, R. (1991). *Child mental health practice from the ecological perspective*. Lanham, MD: University Press of America.

National Center for Education Statistics. (1990). *National education longitudinal study of 1988: The profile of the American eighth grader*. Washington, D.C.: U.S. Government Printing Office.

O'Callaghan, J. (1993). *School-based collaboration with families: Constructing family-school-agency partnerships that work*. San Francisco: Jossey-Bass.

Office of Technology Assessment. (1991). *Adolescent health, Volume I: Summary and policy options* (OTA-H-468). Washington, D.C.: U.S. Government Printing Office.

Pargament, K., & Maton, K. (Eds.). (1991). Religion and prevention in mental health: Conceptual and empirical foundations. [Special Issue] *Prevention in Human Services, 9*(2).

Parke, R. (1978). Children's home environments: Social and cognitive effects. In I. Altman & J. Wohlwill (Eds.), *Human behavior and environment: Advances an theory and research: Vol. 3. Children and environment* (pp. 33-81). New York: Plenum.

Parke, R., & Kellam, S. (Eds.). (1994). *Exploring family relationships with other social contexts*. Hillsdale, NJ: Erlbaum.

Pastore, C., & Newman, I. (1990, February). *Therapeutic in-home emergency services*. Paper presented at the 3rd Annual Research Conference, "System of Care for Children's Mental Health: Building a Research Base," Research and Training Center for Children's Mental Health, Florida Mental Health Institute, Tampa, FL.

Pattison, E. (1981). Introduction: The social network paradigm. *International Journal of Family Therapy, 3*, 241-245.

Paul, J., & Epanchin, B. (1982). *Emotional disturbance in children*. Columbus, OH: Charles E. Merrill.

President's Commission on Mental Health. (1978). *Report of the task panel on community support systems* (Vol. II). Washington, D.C.: U.S. Government Printing Office.

Price, R. (1979). The social ecology of treatment gain. In A. Goodstein & F. Kanfer (Eds.), *Maximizing treatment gains: Transfer enhancement in psychotherapy* (pp. 383-426). New York: Academic Press.

Reisman, J., & Ribordy, S. (1993). *Principles of psychotherapy with children* (2nd ed.). New York: Lexington Books.

Reppucci, N. (1987). Prevention and ecology: Teenage pregnancy, child sexual abuse, and organized youth sports. *American Journal of Community Psychology, 15*, 1-22.

Richardson, R., & Pfeiffenberger, C. (1983). Social support networks for divorced and stepfamilies. In J. Whittaker & J. Garbarino (Eds.), *Social support networks: Informal helping in the human services* (pp. 219-247). Chicago: Aldine.

Roth, R., & Constantine, L. (1995, July). A good PE class makes every student a winner. *APA Monitor, 26*(7), pp. 59-60.

Rueveni, U. (1979). *Networking families in crisis: Intervention strategies for families and social networks*. New York: Human Sciences Press.

Russell, J., & Ward, L. (1982). Environmental psychology. *Annual Review of Psychology, 33,* 651-688.

Salzinger, S., Antrobus, J., & Hammer, M. (1988). *Social networks of children, adolescents, and college students*. Hillsdale, NJ: Erlbaum.

Saxe, L., Cross, T., & Silverman, N. (1988). Children's mental health: The gap between what we know and what we do. *American Psychologist, 43,* 800-807.

Schoenfeld, P. (1984). Network therapy: Clinical theory and practice with disturbed adolescents. *Psychotherapy: Theory, Research and Practice, 21,* 92-100.

Schulman, R. (1979). Environmental interventions. In J. Noshpitz (Ed.), *Basic handbook of child psychiatry* (pp. 300-314). New York: Basic Books.

Schwartzman, J. (Ed.). (1985). *Families and other systems: The macrosystemic context of family therapy*. New York: Guilford Press.

Searcy, S., & Meadows, N. (1994). The impact of social structures on friendship development for children with behavior disorders. *Education and Treatment of Children, 17,* 255-266.

Shinn, M., Wong, N., Smko, P., & Ortiz-Torres, B. (1989). Promoting the well-being of working parents: Coping, social support, and flexible job schedules. *American Journal of Community Psychology, 17,* 31-55.

Speck, R., & Attneave, C. (1973). *Family networks*. New York: Vantage.

Spock, B. (1994). *A better world for our children*. Bethesda, MD: National Press Books.

Stokols, D. (1977). Origins and directions of environment-behavioral research. In D. Stokols (Ed.), *Perspectives on environment and behavior* (pp. 5-38). New York: Plenum.

Stroul, B., & Friedman, R. (1986). *A system of care for children and youth with severe emotional disturbances* (rev. ed.). Washington, D.C.: Georgetown University Child Development Center, CASSP Technical Center.

Swap, S. (1984). Ecological approaches to working with families of disturbing children. In W. O'Connor & B. Lubin (Eds.), *Ecological approaches to clinical and community psychology* (pp. 107-144). New York: Wiley.

Swenson, C. (1979). Social networks, mutual aid, and the life model of practice. In C. Germain (Ed.), *Social work practice: People and environments* (pp. 213-238). New York: Columbia University Press.

Tolsdorf, C. (1976). Social networks, support, and coping: An exploratory study. *Family Process, 15,* 407-418.

Tracy, E., & McDonell, J. (1991). Home based work with families: The environmental context of family intervention. In K. Lewis (Ed.), *Family systems application to social work: Training and clinical practice* (pp. 93-108).

New York: Haworth Press.

Trickett, E., & Schmid, K. (1993). The school as social context. In P. Tolan & B. Cohler (Eds.), *Handbook of clinical research and practice with adolescents* (pp. 173-202). New York: Wiley.

Trulson, M. (1986). Martial arts training: A novel "cure" for juvenile delinquency. *Human Relations, 39,* 1131-1140.

Van Meter, M., Haynes, O., & Kropp, J. (1987). The negative social work network: When friends are foes. *Child Welfare, 66,* 69-75.

Vaux, A., Burda, P., & Stewart, D. (1986). Orientation toward utilization of support resources. *Journal of Community Psychology, 14,* 159-170.

Vincent, T., & Trickett, E. (1983). Preventive interventions and the human context: Ecological approaches to environmental assessment and change. In R. Felner, L. Jason & J. Moritsugu (Eds.), *Preventive psychology* (pp. 67-86). New York: Pergamon.

Wahler, R. (1980). Parent insularity as a determinant of generalization success in family treatment. In S. Salinger, J. Antrobus & J. Glick (Eds.), *The ecosystem of the "sick" child* (pp. 187-199). New York: Academic Press.

Wells, K., & Biegel, D. (Eds.). (1991). *Family preservation services: Research and evaluation.* Newbury Park, CA: Sage.

Wheldall, K., & Yuk Lam, Y. (1987). Seats of learning. *Educational Psychology, 7,* 303-312.

Whittaker, J., & Garbarino, J. (Eds.). (1983). *Social support networks: Informal helping in the human services.* New York: Aldine.

Whittaker, J., & Tracy, E. (1991). Social network intervention in intensive family-based preventive services. *Prevention in Human Services, 9,* 175-185.

Wicker, A. (1973). Undermanning theory and research: Implications for the study of psychological and behavioral effects of excess human populations. *Representative Research in Social Psychology, 4,* 185-206.

Willems, E., (1977). Behavioral ecology. In D. Stokols (Ed.), *Perspectives on environmental and behavior* (pp. 39-68). New York: Plenum.

Wohlwill, J. (1981). *The physical environment and behavior: An annotated bibliography and guide to the literature.* New York: Plenum.

Wright, L., Frost, C., & Wisecarver, S. (1993). Church attendance, meaningfulness of religion, and depressive symptomatology among adolescents. *Journal of Youth and Adolescents, 22,* 559-568.

Yell, M. (1988). The effects of jogging on the rates of selected target behaviors of behaviorally disordered students. *Behavioral Disorders, 13,* 273-279.

Young, T. (1990). Therapeutic case advocacy: A model for interagency collaboration in serving emotionally disturbed children and their families. *American Journal of Orthopsychiatry, 60,* 118-124.

Author Index

A

Apter & Conoley, 1984 183
Apter, 1982 182, 183, 184
Asp & Garbarino, 1983 97

B

Bachman, 1987 96
Barker & Gump, 1964 22, 105
Barker, 1968 105
Bechtel, 1984 37
Becker, 1976 179
Becvar, Becvar, & Bender, 1982 23
Behar et al., 1994 12
Belle, 1988 164
Belle, 1989 86, 95, 98, 141, 142, 143, 158, 161
Bennett, Lingerfelt, & Nelson, 1990 151, 152, 153
Benson, 1991 110, 115
Berndt & Savin-Williams, 1993 157, 158, 160
Bess, 1994 131
Bloom, 1984 181
Bogenschneider et al., 1990 110
Bronfenbrenner 91
Bronfenbrenner, 1979 4, 6, 179, 180, 181, 182, 183, 184
Browne & Francis, 1993 8
Bryant, 1985 142
Burchard & Clarke, 1990 15, 39, 61, 71
Burchard, Burchard, Sewell, & VanDenBurg, 1993 40, 41, 61, 68, 69, 72, 74

C

Caplan, 1974 99, 137, 183
Caplan, 1976 187
Carnegie Council on Adolescent Development, 1992 98, 107, 111, 118, 119, 121, 122, 123, 124, 126, 127, 128, 129
Catalano, 1979 25
Clark, 1988 128, 132
Clark, Zalis, & Sacco, 1982 36
Cochran & Brassard, 1979 139, 140
Cochran, 1993 93
Cochran, Larner, Riley, Gunnarsson, & Henderson, 1990 98, 139, 141, 142, 143, 144, 159
Cohen & Adler, 1986 186
Cohen, Evans, Stokols, & Krantz, 1986 181, 183, 186
Collins & Pancoast, 1976 184
Combrinck-Graham, 1990 24, 31, 32, 122, 138
Conyne & Clark, 1981 21
Cook & Plas, 1984 182
Csikszentmihalyi & Larson, 1984 65, 66, 67, 127
Csikszentmihalyi, Rathunde, & Whalen, 1993 113
Cutler & Madore, 1980 154, 155, 156, 185

D

DeAngelis, 1993 94
Dunst, Trivette, & Deal, 1988 32, 33, 43, 44, 147, 151

E

Epstein & Karweit, 1983 108
Erickson, 1988 107, 115, 124, 133

F

Family Services Research Center, 1995 47
Farbstein & Kantrowitz, 1978 51
Feagans, 1974 180

Felner et al., 1993 29, 30
Fine, 1992 3, 28, 31, 32, 72
Fitzgerald & Illback, 1993 24, 146
Friedman, 1993 47
Fulghum, 1988 55, 57

G

Garbarino, 1982 26, 180, 181
Garrison, 1981 17, 155, 156
Gatti & Colman, 1976 156
Gavin, 1989 119
Germain, 1981 181
Glassner & Freedman, 1979 22
Goldfried & D'Zurilla, 1969 179
Goodhart & Zautra, 1984 103
Gottlieb, 1981 184
Gottlieb, 1983 146, 157, 184, 186
Greenberger & Steinberg, 1986 95, 96
Greenwood, Carta, & Hall, 1988 106
Grinnell, Kyte, & Bostwick, 1981 186
Gump, 1980 181
Gump, 1984 65

H

Haber, 1987 17
Harari & Hosey, 1981 48
Hartman, 1978 54
Heath & McLaughlin, 1991 113, 126
Heller & Monahan, 1977 105, 108
Henggeler & Borduin, 1990 13, 33, 35
Henggeler, 1982 180
Henggeler, 1991 28, 72, 159, 160, 176
Hirsh, 1980 184
Hobbs, 1982 11, 12
Hollister, Edgerton, & Hunter, 1985 57

I

Ianni, 1989 122, 123, 145
Institute for Social Research, 1987 96

J

Jeger & Slotnick, 1982 180, 182, 183
Jeger, Slotnick, & Shure, 1982 186
Jones & Nisbett, 1971 48

K

Kahn & Antonucci, 1980 186
Katz-Leavy, Lourie, Stroul, & Zeigler-Dendy, 1992 39, 40, 42, 43, 47, 102
Kinney et al., 1991 13
Knitzer, Steinberg, & Fleisch, 1990 100
Kozol, 1974 110
Kraft & DeMaio, 1982 35

L

Larson & Kleiber, 1993 89, 90, 91, 109, 110, 111, 113, 114, 119, 123, 127, 129, 130, 131, 132, 134, 138
Larson & Richards, 1989 66
Lee, 1985 20, 85, 183
Leff, 1978 47, 49

M

Maguire, 1991 69, 70, 94, 99, 100, 111, 118, 137, 139, 151
Maluccio, 1981 179
Mannino & Shore, 1984 12, 38
Martin, 1975 21
McConnell, 1977 180
McGovern et al., 1990 44
Medrich, Roizen, Rubin, & Buckley, 1982 88, 89, 91, 92, 93, 94, 110, 116, 117, 118, 131, 132, 133, 162
Meer, 1986 8
Melton, 1995 178
Milardo, 1988 139, 145, 157
Millon, 1981 185
Moos, 1975 186
Moos, 1976 64, 186
Morse, Smith, & Acker, 1978 182, 185
Munger, 1991 18, 178

N

National Center for Education Statistics, 1990 112
National Education Longitudinal Study, 1988 112

Author Index

O

O'Callaghan, 1993 17, 31, 32, 33, 71, 101, 106, 178
Olson, Whitbeck, & Robinson 47

P

Pargament & Maton, 1991 98, 99
Parke & Kellam, 1994 98, 106, 162, 163, 177
Parke, 1978 182
Pastore & Newman, 1990 8
Pattison, 1981 182, 183
Paul & Epanchin, 1982 51
President's Commission on Mental Health, 1978 138
Price, 1979 22

R

Raleigh News & Observer, 1993 107
Reisman & Ribordy, 1993 11
Reppucci, 1987 130
Richardson & Pfeiffenberger, 1983 187
Roth & Constantine, 1995 121
Rueveni, 1979 17, 18
Russell & Ward, 1982 179, 181

S

Salzinger, Antrobus, & Hammer, 1988 88, 140, 158, 162
Salzinger et al., 1988 144, 157
Saxe, Cross & Silverman, 1988 37
Saxe, Cross, & Silverman, 1988 71
Schoenfeld, 1984 185
Schulman, 1979 35
Schwartzman, 1985 13
Searcy & Meadows, 1994 158, 159, 161, 164
Shinn et al., 1989 8
Speck & Attneave, 1973 17
Spock, 1994 88
Stokols, 1977 185
Stroul & Friedman, 1986 38
Swap, 1984 179, 180
Swenson, 1979 37

T

Tolsdorf, 1976 184, 185, 187
Tracy & McDonell, 1991 1, 4, 16, 33, 64, 65, 68, 70, 87, 147, 150
Trickett & Schmid, 1993 2, 3, 32, 44, 71, 72, 73, 74, 149
Trulson, 1986 8

U

United States Office of Technology Assessment, 199 129

V

Van Meter, Haynes, & Kropp, 1987 9
Vaux, Burda, & Stewart, 1986 185
Vincent & Trickett, 1983 181

W

Wahler, 1980 143
Wells & Biegel, 1991 14
Whittaker & Garbarino, 1983 137
Whittaker & Tracy, 1991 177
Wicker, 1973 105
Willems, 1977 50
Wohlwill, 1981 21
Wright, Frost, & Wisecarver, 1993 9, 98, 99, 100
Wynn et al. 121

Y

Young, 1990 15, 16, 187

Subject Index

A

activities (as resources), 109-134
aggression, 8, 165-167
Alaska Youth Initiative (AYI), 15, 39, 40-43
All I Really Need to Know I Learned in Kindergarten, 56-57
alternative care, 57-58
antisocial behavior, 159-161, 162, 165-167
assets, 110

B

Baby and Child Care, 87
bathrooms, 8
Beck Depression Inventory, 99
behavior setting 53, 179 (defined)
behavior sequences, 72
biology, 2

C

case management, 10, 12
Child and Adolescent Service System Program, 38-39
Child Mental Health Practice from the Ecological Perspective, xi
chores, 90
churches, 7, 9, 98-100
clinical environmental intervention, 3 (defined)
clinician, xii (defined)
community service activities, 122-123
community-family network therapy, 154-157
companionship support, 137
competence, 179 (defined)
competence-oriented intervention, 179 (defined)
consultation, 24, 31, 145
continuum of care, xii
crisis planning, 74
cultural relativity, 179 (defined)

D

Darwin, Charles, 25
depression, 9, 96, 168-170
developmental trajectories, 179 (defined)
deviance, 179 (defined)
diagnosis, 64, 71-72
displacement, 91

E

ecological, 179-180 (defined)
ecological consciousness, 46-61
ecological environment, 180 (defined)
ecological therapist, 180 (defined)
ecologists, 180 (defined)
ecology, 180 (defined)
ecology of human development, 4
ecology, 2
eco-map, 53-55, 180 (defined)
ecosystem, 180 (defined)
Ecosystemic Deficit Disorder (EDD), 71
embeddedness, 181 (defined)
empowerment, 43-45
environment, 181 (defined)
environmental competence, 181 (defined)
environmental ecology (defined), 3
environmental ecology therapy, 10, 18, 107
environmental engineering, 181 (defined)
environmental inertia, 181 (defined)
environmental press, 26, 181 (defined)
environmental psychology, 181 (defined)
environmental reconnaissance, 181 (defined)
environmental repertoire, 182 (defined)
Environmental Status Exam, xii, 63-85, 182 (defined)

Subject Index

Environmental Support Plan (ESP), 73-74, 82-84
environmental trajectories, 182 (defined)
esteem support, 137-138
exosystem, 5, 6
extracurricular activities, 106-107

F

facilitative environments, 51-52 (defined)
family, 182 (defined)
Family Services Research Center, 47
family network therapy, 10, 17-18
family preservation, 10, 14
family systems, 10, 12-13
family-school linkage, 105
"flow" experience, 113
foster care, 9, 165-167
friendships, 157-164, 168-170

G

good environments. *See* facilitative environments
goodness of fit, 36, 182 (defined)

H

habitat, 182 (defined)
high-risk behaviors, 128-129
home environment, 87-93
home-based therapy, 10, 16
Homebuilders, 10, 13-14
homework, 89-90
hyperactivity, 173-175

I

in loco parentis, 122
in-home evaluation, 67-68
in-school support, 101-103
indirect influence, 182 (defined)
individual differences, 183 (defined)
Individual Education Plan (IEP), 17, 101-103
individualized services, 10, 14-15, 39-43
informal support systems, 56-58
informational support, 138
institutional environment, 22
institutionalization, 34, 37-39

instrumental support, 137
interdependence, 25, 32
intervener, 183 (defined)
interviewing, 70-71

J

job flexibility, 8
jobs
    adolescents', 95-97
    parents', 97-98

K

kin, 183 (defined)
Kozol, Jonathan, 110

L

life domains, 183 (defined)
life-space, 183 (defined)
life-space structures, 97, 183 (defined)
linear thinking, 49-50

M

macrosystem, 5, 6, 183 (defined)
managed care, xii, 44-45
manning theory, 120, 183 (defined)
meals, 101-102
mental health, 184 (defined)
mesosystem, 5, 6, 184 (defined)
microsystem, 5, 6, 184 (defined)
"mismatched" activity (to foster change), 120
Monitor the Future Program, 95
multiplexity, 144
multisystemic therapy, xii, 10, 13, 47
mutual aid group, 151, 184 (defined)
music, 90-91

N

National Commission on Resources for Youth, 97
National Education Longitudinal Study, 112
natural caregivers, 184 (defined)
natural helper, 184 (defined)
natural support system, 184 (defined)
natural therapy system, 23-24

negative network orientation, 184 (defined)
neighborhoods, 7, 79, 93-95
network, 184 (defined)
network orientation, 185 (defined)
network reserve, 149
network therapy, 185 (defined)
niche, 185 (defined)
normal environments, 60-61
normalization, 61
normative behavior, 185 (defined)

O

observer attribution bias, 48-49, 185 (defined)
optimal environments, 185 (defined)

P

peers, 105, 157-164
people (as resources), 135-164
person-based theories, 1
person-environment fit, 31, 72
personal care, 90
personal network, 54-56
personality, 185 (defined)
physical environment, 21
places (as resources), 86-108
planning-linking conference, 155, 185 (defined)
pluralistic schools, 103
positive network orientation, 185 (defined)
President's Commission on Mental Health, 138
President's Scientific Advisory Committee, 95
prior interventions, 68-69
privacy, 88
progressive conformity, 186 (defined)
prosocial behaviors, 128

R

Re-ED, xii, 10., 11-12
recreation, 8
relativity of disturbance, 50-51
religion, 98-100. *See also* churches
ripple effect, 186 (defined)

S

school misbehavior, 170-172
school-based collaboration, 10, 16-17
schools, 7, 8, 100-108
second-order linkages, 186 (defined)
self-help groups, 151, 186 (defined)
setting, 186 (defined)
    setting change, 22-23
    setting creation, 23
    setting selection, 22
single parenthood, 142-143
skateboarding, 8
social ecology, 186 (defined)
social environment, 21-22
social network, 139, 186 (defined)
social support, 136-154
    age, 141-142
    assessment of, 146-150
    characteristics, 137
    consulting to, 145-157
    cultural aspects, 140-141
    defined, 186
    gender, 141-142
    intervention steps, 150-157
    introduction to, 136-140
    mobility, 141
    parent social networks, 140
    single parenthood, 142-143
social support network, 139, 187 (defined)
Spock, Benjamin, 87
sports, 129-132
strength assessment, 32, 72
supervision, 162-163
support, 187 (defined)
support systems, 187 (defined)
synagogues. *See* religion
system of care, 38-39

T

Tae Kwon Do, 8-9, 27-28
talking, 90
television, 91-93
therapeutic case advocacy, 10, 15-16, 187 (defined)

"thick" description, 65
thrill-seeking. *See* Type-T personality
time-use, 65-67, 88-93. *See also* activities
total-television households, 92
traits, 11
trajectories, 25-30
transitional activities, 111
Troubled and Troubling Child, The, 11
Type-A personality, 119
Type-T personality, 121

W–Z
Web of Life, 25
workplace, 95-98
WRAP Project, 101
"wraparound" services, xii, 14-15. *See also* Alaska Youth Iniative
Yoruba, 140
youth development organizations, 124-131
zookeeping, 20

About the Author

Richard L. Munger is a child psychologist practicing in Asheville, North Carolina. He was formerly Chief of the Child and Adolescent Mental Health Division, Hawaii Department of Health, and Associate Professor of Psychiatry at the John A. Burns School of Medicine, University of Hawaii. His previous books are *Child Mental Health Practice from the Ecological Perspective* and *Changing Children's Behavior Quickly*. He received his Ph.D. in Educational Psychology from the University of Michigan in 1979.